Political Words and Ideas in Islam

Bernard Lewis

Political Words and Ideas in Islam

Bernard Lewis

Markus Wiener Publishers
Princeton

For information write to:
Markus Wiener Publishers
231 Nassau Street, Princeton, NJ 08542
www.markuswiener.com

Library of Congress Cataloging-in-Publication Data

Lewis, Bernard, 1916–
Political words and ideas in Islam/Bernard Lewis.
Includes bibliographical references.
ISBN-13: 978-1-55876-424-8 (hardcover : alk. paper)
ISBN-10: 1-55876-424-0 (hardcover : alk. paper)
ISBN-13: 978-1-55876-473-6 (paperback : alk. paper)
ISBN-10: 1-55876-473-9 (paperback : alk. paper)
1. Islam and politics. 2. Islam and state. 3. Political science—Islamic countries. 4. Religion and politics—Islamic countries. 5. Political science—Terminology. I. Title.
BP173.7.L49 2006
297.2'72—dc22
2006029945

Printed in the United States of America on acid-free paper.

Contents

Preface

The following articles were published over a period of many years in a number of different journals and countries. Their common theme is the political language of Islam—perhaps the most political of all religious cultures. Some of them deal with the political terms used in Muslim documents and discourse, and examine their precise meaning and connotation; others discuss political concepts and ideas, and the language in which they are expressed and discussed by Muslim writers—bureaucrats, theologians and others. They thus provide a deeper level of documentation for the various themes discussed in my earlier book *The Political Language of Islam* (University of Chicago Press, 1988.)

My special thanks are due to Mr. Alan Verskin, a graduate student at Princeton University, for his work in editing this volume-both in preparing it for the press, and seeing it through the press.

Chapter One

"Hukûmet and Devlet"
Government and State

"Hukûmet and Devlet" Government and State

In an essay written in about 1837, the Ottoman statesman Sadık Rıfat Pasha uses the phrase *düvel-i Avrupa hukûmetleri,* in a context where these words clearly mean "the governments of the states of Europe."[1] The words *devlet* and *hukûmet* were already in common use at that time, but the formulation in this phrase, with the implied distinction between the state (*devlet*) as an abstract and permanent embodiment of authority, and the government (*hukûmet*) as the human and impermanent body of persons exercising that authority, is new in Ottoman and therefore in Islamic usage.

The normal word for government in modern Turkish and Arabic is *hukûmet, ḥukūma.* Used in much the same sense as English "government" or French "gouvernement," it is standard and common throughout the Arabic-speaking lands and in Turkey at the present time—so common indeed that in word counts which have been made of modern Arabic prose, *ḥukūma* ranks among the words of most frequent occurrence, ahead of several quite ordinary prepositions.[2] The word is old, and is attested in Arabic from the earliest of times; its use in the sense of "government" however dates only from the 19th century. In classical Arabic usage it was a verbal noun meaning the act or office of adjudication, of dispensing justice.[3] It could be used in this sense irrespective of whether the person so acting was a sovereign, a judge, or merely an arbitrator. The frequently quoted *ḥadīth* that "an hour of justice in *ḥukūma* is better than 60 years of worship"[4] refers clearly to the administration of justice and not—as in some modern interpretations—to the conduct of government.

The root *ḥ.k.m.,* in Arabic and in some other Semitic languages, expresses the related basic notions of judgment and wisdom. In some Semitic languages, notably Hebrew, it is the sense of wisdom that prevailed. In Arabic the sense of wisdom or even knowledge is present, as for example in *ḥakīm,* a sage, and hence a physician, but it is the sense of judgment or adjudication that is most usual. In the course of time, the root came to connote political as well as judicial authority. Under the Seljuqs and later rulers, the term *ḥukūma,* usually in its Persian or Turkish form (*ḥukūmat, hukûmet*), was used to denote the office or function of the governor, *ḥākim,* usually provincial or local. In Ottoman usage, while retaining its judicial connotation, it often occurs in the sense of governorship, i.e., the obtaining, holding, or tenure of office of a governor. By the 17th century the word is in common use in Ottoman texts. In addition to the specialized sense of governorship, it occurs in the more general sense of government or administration, e.g., in the expression *mahall* or *makarr-i hukumet,* meaning the seat of government or administrative center of a country or province. It is also used when discussing different types or forms of government, abroad as for example in Kâtib Çelebi's discussion of the different types of government or regime prevailing in Europe, namely monarchy, aristocracy and democracy.[5]

By the end of the 18th century, we find the word *ḥukūma/hukûmet* used in both Turkish and Arabic in a wider and more general sense of rule, of exercising authority. It appears in this sense in the Arabic version of a letter sent by General Menou to the Diwan in Cairo, in January 1801, in which he is described as representative of the authority of the French republic (*muẓāhir ḥukūmatihā*).[6] The term also occurs in some early Turkish and Arabic translations of European historical writings, in the broad sense of rule, dominion, political authority, or even regime.[7] Though common in early 19th century Turkish, the use of the word in this sense in Arabic remains comparatively rare. The Arabic translation of Machiavelli's *Prince*, made in 1824–25, does not use the word *ḥukūma* for government, but prefers such words as *siyāda* and even *amīriyya*.[8] Shaykh Rifā'a Rāfi' al-Ṭahṭāwī, in his Arabic translation of the French constitutional charter, renders the word "gouvernement" by *tadbīr al-mamlaka*.[9]

The present-day meaning—government, in the sense of the group of men exercising the authority of the State—seems to date from the second quarter of the 19th century. The changeover is gradual. Thus Sadık Rıfat Pasha, who wrote a number of political memoranda and essays, habitually uses the word *hukûmet* in the earlier sense of type of government, administration or regime. However, in the essay cited above, he uses it in a context which clearly indicates the modern meaning. The distinction he makes between the State (*dawla, devlet*) and the government (*ḥukūma, hukûmet*) thereafter becomes increasingly common in both Arabic and

Turkish, though the use of the term in the earlier, more abstract, sense continued for some time.[10]

In modern Turkish and Arabic the distinction between *dawla* and *ḥukūma* is clear and general, and usage does not differ greatly from that of English or French. In Persian the change came somewhat later. During the 19th and much of the 20th century, *dawlat* was used indiscriminately for both the state and the government, no clear distinction being made between the two either as concepts or as terms. The earlier Arabic loan word *ḥukūmat* was used in the general sense of political authority and sometimes of administration. Since the 1930's, there has been a tendency by Persian journalists to use the term *ḥukūmat* in the Anglo-French or Turko-Arabic sense but this is still far from general.

The word *dawla*, by far the most widely used in Islamic languages in the sense of state or government, seems to date as a political term from the accession to power of the Abbasids. It comes of course from the Arabic root *d.w.l.*, which has parallels in other Semitic languages and which has the basic meaning of to rotate, turn, change, alternate, or to succeed one another, as for example when speaking of the seasons. The noun *dawla* is attested at a very early stage in Arabic in the sense of turn, meaning not only a rotation, but something rather like the idiomatic English use of the word. In the Qur'ān (iii, 140) we find the verbal form *nudāwiluhā* "we cause them to alternate," speaking of the good days and the bad days, and there are many passages in ancient Arabic poetry in which the word *dawla* has the meaning of someone's turn at success, power or good fortune. The word *dawla* is in common use in both *ḥadīth* and early poetry in the sense of turn. It is not limited to the more familiar meaning of someone's turn at success or power but is used more generally, as for example of a wife's "turn," in a polygamous household, with her husband. The form *dūlatan* occurs in the Qur'ān (lix, 7) in the sense of something which is held in common, i.e., the ownership of which is passed around a number of persons. These and similar expressions are based on the underlying image of the wheel of fortune, the slowly turning wheel which brings one man or group up and another down. It is, of course, an image which long antedates Islam and of which probably the best known classical exposition is that of the Greek author Polybius. Polybius, at discussing revolution (*anakyklosis*), describes the slowly turning wheel driven by the force of *tyche*, fortune, and its expression in the cycle of political changes which follow and repeat one another.[11] Kingship leads to tyranny, tyranny breaks down into aristocracy, aristocracy gives rise to oligarchy, oligarchy splinters into democracy, democracy degenerates into mob rule, mob rule brings men back to the state of nature, out of which a new kingship emerges and a new cycle begins. This idea reappears in Islamic literature at a later date with some variation in the terms, and *dawla* is the word used for the turning of the wheel.

The word *dawla* occurs a number of times in works written by or attributed to Ibn al-Muqaffaʿ. In a well known passage in the *Ṣaḥāba*, he refers to the accession of the Abbasids in the phrase ثمّ كانت هذه الدولة [12] Pellat is certainly right in reading this not as "then came this dynasty" but rather as "then came this change" (*changement, revirement*). This interpretation is confirmed by several other occurrences in these texts. Thus in a passage in the *Adab Ṣaghīr*, we find the phrase "*al-dunya duwal*".[13] In the context it is clear that Ibn al-Muqaffa' does not mean that the world consists of dynasties or states, as the phrase would mean in modern Arabic. His meaning is that the world is full of ups and downs, of vicissitudes, and he continues to say: "what is for you will come to you despite your weakness; what is against you cannot be averted by your strength." In a passage in the *Adab Kabīr* the writer draws his reader's attention to certain differences in the situation at the beginning of a new regime إذا كان سلطانك عند جدّة دولة.[14] This may be understood to mean: If your rule or power occurs at the beginning of a new turn or phase or regime.

An interesting example of the use of the term occurs in the text of a sermon delivered in Mecca in the year 130/747–8 by a Kharijite rebel, and preserved by several authors. The speaker is at pains to inform his listeners, the people of Medina, that he and his companions did not leave their homes and their possessions in a spirit of wantonness or folly or frolic, nor ولا لدولة ملك نريد أن نأخذ فيه ولا لثار قديم نيل منّا[15] a phrase which appears to mean neither in quest of new dominion nor in search of old vengeance.

These and similar passages make it easier to interpret the term *dawla* as used in the early Abbasid period. When Ṭabarī and other historians of the Abbasids describe the Caliph Ṣaffāḥ and others speaking of *dawlatunā*, our *dawla*, they do not mean "our state," nor do they mean "our dynasty." They mean "our turn." The implication is that the Umayyads have had their turn and now it is the Abbasids' turn. This is confirmed by the early texts in which the same word *dawla* is used of persons who are not sovereigns and do not found dynasties. Saffāḥ for example in one of his speeches is reported as speaking of "the *dawla* of Abū Muslim"[16] i.e., of the time when

Abū Muslim was so to speak on the upturn of the wheel. Other passages speak of the *dawla* of the Barmakids. The term is used several times in connection with Abū Muslim. Thus, discussing the number of people killed by Abū Muslim in the course of his activities, Ṭabarī uses the phrase *fī dawlatihi wa-ḥurūbihi.*[17] This would seem to mean something like "in the course of his career and his wars." In another passage quoted by Ṭabarī from Madā'inī, Abū Muslim himself is quoted as using the word in a very revealing context. Discussing which are more valiant, the Syrians or the Khurasanis, Abū Muslim remarks كلّ قوم في دولتهم اشدّ الناس—every people is the most valiant of mankind at the time of its "turn" i.e., when it is on the upturn of the wheel.[18]

Since the accession of the Abbasids was the *dawla* par excellence, the word came to mean the Abbasid dynasty, which had a rather longer turn than any other, and then more generally the Abbasid state. We find it for example in such expressions as *abnā' al-dawla,* literally the sons of the *dawla,* meaning certain groups of persons adopted into the service of *dawla; 'arab al-dawla,* the Arab tribes in the service of the *dawla.* Later it comes to mean the state or the dynasty more generally, and not merely the reigning Abbasid house.

Even as late as the 10th century, when the word *dawla* had become fairly standardized in the meaning of dynasty or state, we still encounter it in the earlier sense. Thus the authors of the *Rasā'il Ikhwān al-Ṣafā,* presenting a cyclical theory of political regimes, uses the word dawla commonly in this sense. The affairs of this world are دول ونوب تدور بين أهلها قرناً بعد قرن ومن امّة الى امّة ومن بلد الى بلد.[19]

The titulature of sovereigns and of lesser rulers is a good indication. In this *dawla* is often associated with *mulk,* kingship, and contrasted with *dīn,* religion. The best titles are the paired ones-indicating that the holder of the title holds a position in relation to *al-dawla wa'l-dīn,* which comes to mean of the state and of the faith. Such titles already contain the beginnings of the idea that these are two themes, contrasted or complementary. Titles in *al-dawla* and *al-dīn* were much used by the Buyids and their successors, probably because they felt it necessary to use something with a connotation of real authority. Titles in *al-dawla* were also used by the Fatimids in Egypt and granted by them to their viziers and other functionaries. We find the word *dawla* being used by dynasties of themselves, usually with some honorific adjective. Thus the Fatimids were *al-dawla al-hādiya,* the rightly guided dynasty. In Egypt the Ayyubids used the formula *al-dawla al-'aliya,* the lofty or sublime or exalted dynasty. This was in due course taken over by the Ottomans and became their standard way of referring to themselves—*devlet-i 'aliye-i osmaniye,* the high Ottoman state or dynasty. By Ottoman times we also find the word *dawla* (Turkish *devlet*) used of foreign states and even of infidel states in Europe. By this time the word *dawla* in the sense of state or dynasty has a plural as well as a singular form. Indeed the usual term for foreign states in Ottoman administrative usage is *duvel-i ecnebiye.* In other words, *dawla/devlet* has become the normal word for the state. It may be noted that it is however in the main limited to practical and administrative use. The word is not much used in theoretical discussions of the state, whether in the juridical or in the philosophical literature, the authors of which still prefer to use other terms when discussing the acquisition and exercise of political authority.

Chapter Two

"Serbestiyet"

Freedom

"Serbestiyet"
Freedom

The first great Ottoman reform edict, the «Rescript (*Hatt-i Şerif*) of the Rose-Bower (Gülhane) of 1839, contains the following clause: «Everyone shall possess and dispose of his possessions and his property in complete freedom (*kemal-i serbestiyette*), without interference from any quarter». Later in the same document, in a reference to judicial council meetings, the desire is expressed that those attending such meetings should state their opinions and observations freely (*serbestçe*).[1]

The word *serbestiyet,* rendered "freedom," attracted some attention at the time. The French dragoman and orientalist Belin, in a contemporary comment, noted that "Le mot سربستيت *ser-bestiyyet* est un des mots que les Turcs ont introduit nouvellement dans leur langue, quoique le primitif y existât déjà. II dérive de سربست *ser-best,* adjectif composé persan, que signifie libre, auquel on a ajouté le ى pour en faire un nom abstrait; puis les Turcs l'ont, pour ainsi dire, arabisé, en ajoutant un *teche-dyd* sur le *ye*, et le faisant suivre d'un *hé*."[2] A recent writer has gone even further, and has claimed that the Gülhane Rescript was the first document in the Ottoman Empire in which the word "serbestiyet" was used, and that this word was «a Turkish neologism invented on the occasion to convey the French 'liberté' ».

In fact, neither the word nor the notion was new to the Ottomans, nor is this the first document in which it appears. As has already been pointed out elsewhere,[3] the word occurs in the Turkish text of the Treaty of Küçük Kaynarca of 1774, a document of some importance in Ottoman history. By the terms of this treaty the Ottomans were compelled to relinquish their suzerainty over the Crimean Tatars who were granted a brief and rather formal independence as a preliminary to their annexation to the Russian Empire a few years later. While the clause was in fact little more than a face-saving device for the Ottoman sultan, it is of some interest as a document in the development of political thought and language. By the terms of the treaty, both the Czar and the Sultan agreed to recognize the Crimean Tatars as «free and entirely independent of any foreign power». The Sultan was to be recognized by the Tatars as «Grand Caliph of Muhammedanism», but this recognition was to be purely religious, and was agreed «without thereby compromising their political and civil liberty as established». The treaty is extant in Turkish and French, but appears to have been originally drafted in Italian. The form of words in the Italian text for these two phrases are: «liberi, immediati, ed independenti assolutamente da qualunque straniera Potenza..» and «senza pero mettere in compromesso la stabilita libertà loro politica e civile». In the first phrase the Turkish text reads: «serbestiyet ve gayr-i taalluk mustakıl vücuhla ecnebi bir devlete tâbi olmamak üzre»; in the second: «akdolunan serbestiyet-i devlet ve memleketlerine halel getirmiyerek..."».[4]

The Ottoman Dragoman who in 1774 chose the word *serbestiyet* as equivalent for freedom was not creating a neologism, any more than the draftsman of the «Rescript of the Rose Bower» in 1839. The words *serbest,* free, and *serbestiyet,* freedom, were already in current use in 18th century Turkish with an unmistakably political meaning, indeed far more so than in the Rescript, where *serbestçe* and *serbestiyet* are used in contexts of judicial debate and of property, not of civil or political rights. But such usage had long been normal in Turkish. At a time when the Arabic loanwords *hür* and *hürriyet,* free and freedom, still retained their primarily legal meaning—i.e., free in the sense of not being a slave—*serbest* and *serbestiyet* were already clearly political.

A few examples may suffice. The famous Ambassador Yirmisekiz Çelebi Mehmed Said Efendi, who went to France in 1720, notes in the course of his itinerary visits to the «free cities» (*serbest şehir*) of Toulouse and Bordeaux. Not content with merely using this term, he explains what it means. Each city was the seat of a *parlement* and *president.* Both words are given in French, transcribed in the Turko-Arabic script, and are explained. The Ambassador notes that these cities have the valuable privilege of being garrisoned only by their own levies and not having royal troops stationed in them.[5] Another free city, Danzig, is also described in an early 18th century Turkish treatise on the states and governments of Europe.[6]

By the latter part of the 18th and early 19th centuries, the word *serbestiyet* appears to have been in common use. Thus, the Ambassador Azmi Efendi, who passed through Hungary in 1790 on his way to Berlin, notes that the previous Emperor Joseph deprived the Hungarians of their «ancient liberties» (*kadimi serbestiyetler*), but that the reigning Emperor Leopold had restored them.[7]

The Ottoman Ambassador in Paris under the *Directoire,* Moralı Esseyid Ali Efendi, speaks of *serbestiyet* in his report,[8] while the Chief Secretary Atıf Efendi, in his important memorandum written in 1798 to examine the political situation created by the revolution in France and the activities of the revolutionary government, uses the word several times—first to describe the basic ideas of the French revolutionaries and their commitment to equality and freedom (*musavat ve serbestiyet*) and then, in a context of more immediate concern, in describing French propaganda among the Greeks and their attempt to install «a form of liberty» (*serbestiyet*) in the Greek islands and mainland towns which they had occupied.[9]

By the early 19th century the word was already in use in Turkey in domestic contexts. Thus, the historian Şanizade, who died in 1826, gives an extremely interesting and important description of the principles of consultation (*meşveret*) and the way in which such consultations should be conducted. A point of some significance is that the discussion in these assemblies should be free (*ber vech-i serbestiyet*).[10] In the forms *serbestiyet* and *serbesti,* the term passed into common Ottoman usage in the 19th century and remained the normal expression for political freedom until it was replaced first by *hürriyet,* now given a political rather than a legal context, and subsequently by *özgürlük.*

What is the origin of the term? Etymologically, the word *serbest* is Persian, and means, among other things, exempt, untrammelled, unrestricted. It may be used of an individual acting independently, but does not normally have a political connotation in Persian, which prefers *âzâd* and its derivatives in this sense. *Serbestî* is a Persian abstract form; *serbestiyet* is an Ottoman pseudo-Arabic creation, unknown to either Persian or Arabic usage. In classical Ottoman usage the normal meaning of *serbest* was neither legal nor political but fiscal. It was used to indicate the absence of normal limitations and restrictions. It most commonly appears in connection with *timars,* the grants of revenues assigned to the *sipahis,* the feudal cavalry. Normally while most of the revenues were allocated to the recipient of a *timar,* certain revenues, as for example the poll-tax on non-Muslims, were reserved to the Imperial treasury. A *serbest timar* was one untrammelled by any such restrictions or limitations, in which therefore all the revenues went to the assignee and none were retained by the Imperial treasury.[11] The use of the term in the Rescript of 1839 is thus directly related to its earlier fiscal and financial usage. It is interesting and significant that when called upon to discuss political freedom as that expression was understood in Europe, the Ottomans should have had recourse to a word with practical and administrative significance rather than have drawn on the vocabulary of philosophy or law. It was a good basis on which to build.

Chapter Three

"Meşveret"
Consultation

"Meşveret" Consultation

The term *meşveret*, consultation, was much used by the young Ottomans and by later Turkish exponents of the idea of constitutional and representative government. It occurs frequently in particular in the writings of Namık Kemal, who has even been credited, mistakenly, with having coined the word as a Turkish equivalent for representative government.

In fact neither the word nor the political concept that it denotes was new, either in Ottoman or indeed in Islamic history. The notion of consultation as an obligation of the ruler goes back to the advent of Islam; the attempt to organize some sort of apparatus of consultation goes back at least a thousand years in the history of the Turkish people.

The practice of consultation and deliberation was already familiar in pre-Islamic Arabia, as is attested by Arabic references to the meetings of bodies, variously called *majlis* and *mala*,[1] as well as in some old South Arabian inscriptions. Two verses in the Qur'ān, Chapter III, 153/159 and XLII, 36/38 are frequently cited as imposing a duty of consultation on rulers. Consultation (*mashwara* and *mushāwara*) is contrasted with arbitrary personal rule (*istibdād*). The former is recommended, the latter is deplored. The case in favor of consultation is supported by a considerable body of material—by traditionists, recording the precept and practice of the Prophet[2]; by commentators, elaborating on the two above named verses in the Qur'ān[3]; by numerous later writers, in Arabic, Persian and Turkish, belonging to both the legal and scribal traditions.[4] In general, the *ulema* urged the need for consultation with the *ulema*, the bureaucrats were more insistent on the importance of consulting bureaucrats.

However, while consultation was recommended and arbitrary personal rule deplored, the one was not enjoined nor the other forbidden. In the early Islamic centuries, there seems to have been no formal procedure whereby the ruler consulted with his advisors, of whatever category. As H.A.R. Gibb remarked, commenting on some modern attempts to read parliamentary procedures into early Islamic history: "There is, in fact, nothing in the texts to justify the suggestion that 'Umar's consultation was more than informal, or that there was at Medina any recognized consultative committee, still less a cabinet."[5] The nearest approach to a consultative body was the famous committee appointed by the Caliph 'Umar on his deathbed, with the function of choosing one of themselves as his successor in the caliphate.[6] The Umayyad caliphs, at least the earlier ones, seem to have continued the old Arabian practice of consultation with the elders of the tribes through the so-called delegations (*wufūd*).[7] But the trend of events was towards greater, not lesser personal authority in the sovereign or his agents. The increasingly authoritarian character of government is vividly expressed in a passage quoted by several Arab authors. A certain Sudayf, a dependent of the Hashimites, is cited as complaining of the changes resulting from the supersession of the Umayyads by the Abbasids: "By God, our booty, which was shared, has become a perquisite of the rich; our leadership, which was consultative (*mashwara*), has become arbitrary; our succession, which was by the choice of the community, is now by inheritance."[8]

The medieval scribal and legal traditions, though generally in favor of consultation, are not uniformly so. While approving it in the abstract, some authors seem to have been somewhat alarmed by examples which they encountered in practice. Without formally condemning consultation as such, they sometimes indicate that in excess it may lead to anarchy and destruction. Thus no less an authority than the 11th century Spanish Arab scholar Ibn Ḥazm, in discussing the question of succession to rule, remarks that the election of a successor by consensus (*ijmāʿ*) or even by committee (*shūrā*) can lead to anarchy. Ibn Ḥazm was no doubt impressed by the quarrels and disputes amid which the great caliphate of Cordova came to an end.[9] Another harsh judgment on democracy in action is given by the Egyptian scholar Qalqashandī. Speaking of the city of Sis in Anatolia, he notes that «authority became consultative (*mashwara*), the populace became anarchic, the fortifications fell into disrepair», and the city thus fell prey to Christian conquest.[10]

A different kind of judgment, though equally negative, occurs in a book by the Arab traveller Ibn Faḍlān, who visited the Turkish Bulgars of the Volga in 309/921. Describing their form of government, he notes that it was consultative, and indeed uses the words of the Qur'anic verse III, 153/159, "*wa-amruhum shūrā baynahum*," to describe it. Despite the Qur'ānic authority which he cites, Ibn Faḍlān makes it clear that he does not like this form of government, observing that whenever these people are able to agree among themselves on anything, their decision is nullified by «the meanest and lowest among them».[11]

With the invasion of the Middle East by the steppe peoples, first Turks and then Mongols, we begin to find references, for the first time in Islamic history, to regular and permanent consultative councils. The Ilkhans in Persia appear to have adhered to the practice of convening a great council of high dignitaries, presided over by the vizier. This body, known in Persian as the *dīvān-i buzurg,* may be based on the Mongol tribal council, the *kurultay.* Such a council continued to exist under the post-Mongol rulers of Persia. The name often given to it, *janqi,* would appear to indicate a Mongol origin.[12] The functioning of this body is attested by both Persian and external sources. Among the latter we may mention the Ottoman historian Kemalpaşazade, who, discussing the eastern campaigns of the Ottoman Sultan Mehmed II, refers to the holding of such a council in Persia. When, he says, the Persian monarch received a report from a spy that the Ottoman sultan and his army were moving eastward, he summoned a meeting of "the dignitaries of his state and the notables of his realm and consulted with them."[13] In Egypt too, under the Baḥrī Mamluks, there seems to have been a supreme council of high ranking emirs.[14] Though Egypt was never conquered by the Mongols, it was ruled for centuries by a military elite recruited principally from the Turks and other steppe peoples, and the practice of the Mamluk state and army reflect in many ways the influence of the Mongols, then the dominant power in the Middle East.

Under the later Circassian Mamluks, this council seems to have faded away; at least references to it in the sources are extremely rare.

Perhaps the most striking instance of *meşveret* in medieval times may be found in some accounts of the Ottoman state and dynasty. According to an early historiographic tradition, the establishment of the House of Osman took place in this way. The beys and *kethudas* of that region met together, went to Osman Bey, and held a council. After much discussion they chose Osman, and asked him to become their chief. He accepted.[15] This may or may not be an authentic account of the birth of the Ottoman state. But even if it is a myth, the fact that early Ottoman chroniclers should have chosen this kind of myth and enshrined it in the dynastic historiography is in itself of great significance.

Ottoman, like earlier Islamic authors, urged the importance of consultation by the ruler. In the Ottoman empire such was indeed the practice. The high council (*dīwān-i humāyūn*) was an important part of the Ottoman governmental system. Presided over in earlier times by the Sultan, in later times by the Grand Vizier, it had a prescribed membership, prescribed times of meeting, and a regular order of business. The term *meşveret* however was not commonly used of this high council, but rather to denote *ad hoc* meetings and assemblies of military and other dignitaries, summoned to consider problems as they arose. There are frequent references to such *meşverets* in the course of the wars in Europe in the 15th century. They continued to be common in the Ottoman chronicles of the 16th, 17th and 18th centuries. Naima for example offers many accounts of military *meşverets* convened in the field by commanders, as well as of civilian gatherings held in Istanbul by official dignitaries. Towards the end of the 18th century such gatherings became much more frequent, especially in the periods of crisis associated with the Russian and other wars.[16]

A new phase began with the accession of Selim III who at the very beginning of his reign convened a consultative assembly (*meşveret*) of leading officials to discuss the problems of the empire and the way to remedy them. Such gatherings were often held under Selim III and his successors, in the provinces as well as in the capital.[17]

By this time the practice of *meşveret* had acquired a new reality, because of the growing strength of the limiting powers in the Ottoman system. There were several of these. One was of course the *ulema*, a well entrenched body which enjoyed financial independence through their control of the large estates which were held as *vaqf* and which they administered; they also enjoyed authority deriving from popular recognition. They were thus in a position of comparative independence in relation to the Sultan.

A second limiting group consisted of the notables and local dynasts, the *ayan* and *derebeys*, a kind of local magistracy and gentry with a considerable measure of autonomy. Like the medieval English barons, they tried to formalize their rights and privileges against the monarchy. In 1807 they attempted to demarcate their powers, and in 1808 succeeded in imposing on Mahmud II, newly succeeded to the Sultanate, the famous Deed of Agreement which set forth in detail a regulated contractual limitation of the sultan's powers.[18]

It did not last. The 19th century, with the new and effective means of surveillance and repression which it offered, was not a good time for a Turkish Magna Charta.

Nevertheless these ideas were in the air. The Ottoman historian Şanizade, who died in 1826, speaks of consultative meetings held at the Ottoman court, and says: «Her bir tedbir-i umur-i mülkiyeleri hademe-i devlet ve vükela-i raiyyetten ibaret iki sınıf erbab-i meşveret meyanında ber vech-i serbestiyet bahis ü münazara ile karargir ve hükmü agleb her ne vechile netice olup olursa... tenfir». This is a remarkably interesting passage, which contains a whole series of radically new ideas.[19]

Şanizade's account marks the transtition from a purely traditional Islamic interpretation of *meşveret* to a new approach influenced by the practice of European states, to which indeed he alludes under the polite euphemism «well-organized states». He may possibly have been thinking of the British parliament, a description of which, by the young Ottoman diplomatist Mahmud Raif, was available to him in Istanbul.[20] Şanizade notes that the holding of such *meşverets* was common in these states, and that they served a useful purpose. At the same time he was naturally concerned to justify the holding of such meetings with both Islamic and Ottoman precedents.

Probably the earliest use of the term in an explicitly Western context occurs in the Turkish translation of the first volume of Carlo Botta's *History of Italy from 1789 to 1814.* This was first printed in Cairo in Turkish as *Bonapart Tarihi* in 1249/1833, and later reprinted in Istanbul. In this work the term *"parlamento" meşvereti* is used to describe the parliamentary regimes established by the Italian liberals.[21]

In the course of the 19th century the term was much used by Turkish and Arabic authors, first to describe European representative institutions as these became known to them, and then to justify their introduction at home. Thus the Egyptian Sheikh Rifā'a Rāfi' al-Ṭahṭāwī, who spent the years 1826–1831 in Paris, in discussing the functioning of the French parliamentary system, makes common use of the term *mashwara* to describe the various consultative bodies.[22] His book was published in a Turkish translation as well as in the original Arabic and provided readers of both languages with their first detailed and documented account of constitutional and representative government as practiced in a west European country. By the time the term was adopted by the young Ottoman liberal patriots in the mid-century, it was already an accepted part of Ottoman usage.

Chapter Four

“Siyāsa”
Politics

"Siyāsa" Politics

The word *siyāsa,* according to the Arabic dictionary, is derived from the root *sāsa/yasūsu,* the primary meaning of which is to manage, tend or train animals, more particularly horses. The Arabic verb is of course related to the biblical Hebrew substantive *sūs*, a horse, which also occurs in slightly variant forms in other ancient Semitic languages, although the root itself is probably of non-Semitic origin. The word has even found its way into English in the form syce, an Anglo-Indian term meaning a groom, one who looks after horses, from the Arabic active participle *sā'is.*[1]

The earliest Arabic use of the term is *siyāsat al-khayl,* looking after or managing horses. The English word 'manage,' incidentally, itself originally denotes the handling and training of a horse (cf. French *manège* from Italian *maneggio,* a riding school). The subsequent extension of the meaning of the term 'management' in Western languages, however, has been administrative and commercial rather than political. For the latter we have preferred to use a different image, that embodied in the word government, from the Greek κυβερναν, to steer, cf. κυβερνητης, a steersman or helmsman. It is natural that the maritime peoples of the West should draw their imagery of politics from the steering and running of a ship, as the Arabs from the training and use of a horse.

Siyāsa, which we usually translate as 'politics,' could perhaps be more appropriately rendered in English as 'statecraft.' As normally used in classical Arabic, it denotes a skill or a craft rather than a doctrine or a philosophy. The metaphor implied in this use of the Arabic word *siyāsa* is stated explicitly by the eighth-century Arab author 'Abd al-Ḥamīd al-Kātib in his letter to secretaries, an important text reflecting the corporate ethos of the bureaucratic classes and written before the end of the Umayyad dynasty:

> For you know that the man who handles a beast, if he is perceptive in his task, will try to understand the beast's character. If it kicks, he takes care of its rear legs; if it rears, he watches its forelegs; if it bolts, he does not spur it when he rides; if he fears that it will bite, he keeps a watch on its head; if it is stubborn, he curbs its caprices gently on the way; if it persists, he turns it slightly to the side so that it becomes easier to guide. In this description of the care of beast, there are also indications for those who handle men and who manage, test and have dealings with them.[2]

In 'Abd al-Ḥamīd's text, *siyāsa* appear as an image, a parallel. Before very long, however, *siyāsa* is used fairly commonly in the sense of statecraft, the manner of governing, or the ability to govern. If we may accept the textual accuracy of certain early historical narratives—admittedly a large assumption—the term *siyāsa* was already in use during the time of the Caliph 'Umar.

Thus for example we are told that the Caliph dismissed 'Ammār ibn Yāsir because of a complaint that he was "weak, with no knowledge of *siyāsa*."[3] Similarly, in a letter allegedly written by the Caliph 'Umar to his governor 'Amr, he speaks of his expectation of "your good government."[4]

The word *siyāsa* occurs frequently, in the sense of statecraft, in statements or dicta attributed to the Umayyad period. There are numerous sayings ascribed to Umayyad Caliphs and princes in the works of Ibn Qutayba and other collectors of similar literary materials. These can of course easily represent an anachronistic use of terms which only become current at a later date. Somewhat better evidence may be found in the texts of letters, speeches and poems. These, although their authenticity and dating are also open to question, may cumulatively offer a more reliable indication.

A few examples may suffice. In a speech placed in the mouth of Ziyād, the governor of Iraq at the time of Mu'āwiya, we find the words *nasūsukum bi-sulṭāni 'llāhi 'l-ladhi a'ṭānā*—"We govern you by the authority of God which He has given us."[5] An allegedly contemporary report on the appointment of Naṣr ibn Sayyār as governor of Khurāsān in A.H. 120/A.D. 741 says that he was chosen because he was the most manly of the Arabs and the most skilled in statecraft (*a'lamuhum bi'l-siyāsa*).[6] In the course of the events which led to the fall of the Umayyads and the accession of the Abbasids, poets use the term *siyāsa* both to condemn the bad government of the old rulers and to express the hope for good government by the new. The Umayyad prince 'Abbās ibn Walīd warns his kinsmen of the widespread discontent with their misrule:

> I bid you take refuge with God from seditions
> Which rise up like mountains and then collapse
> People have grown weary of your government (*siyāsatukum*).[7]

In contrast, other poets, favorable to the Abbasid pretenders, have better expectations. 'Ajjāj awaits a Caliph who will "govern (*sāsa*) without arrogance,"[8] while Kumayt speaks of an almost messianic ruler-to-come of the house of Hāshim, whose government would be acceptable [to God].[9]

Sometimes the word is used in a somewhat more military context. Balādhurī, for example, speaks in one place of a man "without knowledge of warfare or the *siyāsa* of men," in another of one "without knowledge of warfare or the *siyāsa* of affairs."[10] The poet Mujāhid al-Minqarī, whom he quotes elsewhere, is more explicit and speaks of having commanded (*sūstu*) armies.[11]

Another example of the use of the term *siyāsa* in a military sense occurs in a passage in Hilāl who quotes the Vizier 'Alī ibn 'Īsā as saying that the vizierate required a fully competent scribe able to run affairs (*mumshin li'l-umūr*) and knowing the running of the army (*siyāsat al-jund*).[12]

Such usage is uncommon, however, and the normal meaning is exclusively political. Some passages in Ibn Qutayba even ascribe definitions of the term to prominent Umayyad figures. Prince Walīd asked his father: "What is *siyāsa*?" The Caliph 'Abd al-Malik replied: "*Siyāsa* means to win the respect and sincere affection of the upper classes, to bind the hearts of the common people by dealing justly with them, and to be patient with the lapses of your underlings." "The most politic of kings (*aswas al-mulūk*)," he goes on to say "is he who binds the bodies of his subjects to his obedience through their hearts."[13]

The term is similarly used in an old Persian dictum frequently repeated by Arabic writers which says, with minor variants, "There is no authority (*sulṭān*) without men, no men without money, no money without prosperity, no prosperity without justice and good government (*ḥusn al-siyāsa*). Another popular dictum frequently occurring in early texts says: "Govern (*sus*) the best of men through love; for the common people mix expectation and fear; for the worst of mankind rule through terror."[14]

By early Abbasid times we find the term *siyāsa* in common use in the sense of statecraft, not only in general narratives or discussions by later writers but also, with increasing frequency, in verses or utterances attributed to specific individuals. The first Abbasid Caliph, al-Saffāḥ, in his inaugural speech delivered at Kufa in about A.H. 132/A.D. 749 is quoted as condemning those who believe that anyone else has a better claim to "the headship, the *siyāsa*, and the Caliphate" than the Abbasids.[15]

The term *siyāsa* is used frequently in connection with the Caliph al-Manṣūr. Thus al-Mas'ūdī credits him with good administration and sound statecraft (*ṣawāb al-tadbīr wa-ḥusn al-siyāsa*) beyond all description, while Ya'qūbī quotes him as enjoining his successor to adopt "a virtuous life and good statecraft" (*al-sīra al-ḥasana wa'l-siyāsa al-jamīla.*).[16] Of Hārūn al-Rashīd, on the contrary, al-Mas'ūdī remarks that things went wrong after the affair of the Barmakids and that his maladministration and misgovernment (*qubḥ tadbīrihi wa-sū' siyāsatihi*) became apparent to the people.[17]

The word occurs several times in a dated document. In a letter sent by Ṭāhir to his son in A.H. 205/A.D. 801, when the latter became governor, he advises him; "make use in your duties of men with judgment, skill, experience, knowledge of *siyāsa* and sobriety. And if you behave well, you in your turn will be praised for your statecraft (*takūn maḥmūd al-siyāsa*)."[18]

The poet Abu'l-Ma'āfī, addressing the Lady Khayzurān, the mother of the Caliph al-Hādī, urges her to relax and "let your two sons govern the subjects."[19] The Caliph al-Hādī in turn is quoted as saying to his mother, on his deathbed: "I have forbidden certain things to you and imposed other things on you, in accordance with the requirements of the statecraft of kingship (*siyāsat al-mulk*) and not the prescriptions of the holy law."[20] Al-Hādī's last words, contrasting kingship with holy law, indicate a significant new development in the use of the term *siyāsa* which was in time to change radically its common use and acceptation.

A foreshadowing of the new usage, and more specifically of the doctrine which it represents, may be found in one of the key texts of Islamic political thought, the *Risāla fi'l-ṣaḥāba* of Ibn al-Muqaffa', who died in about A.H. 140/A.D. 757. Ibn al-Muqaffa' appears to use the actual word *siyāsa* only once in this text when, in discussing the ill effects of Umayyad maladministration, he accuses the fallen regime's viziers and secretaries of conducting themselves in an evil manner harmful to reputation, good-breeding and statecraft (*siyāsa*), such as to attract the evil and to repel the good.[21] Without, however, using the term, Ibn al-Muqaffa' does provide the first sketch of a theoretical justification of the new meaning that the word *siyāsa* subsequently acquired. He does not directly challenge the growing authority of the fundaments of the *sharīʿa, Qur'ān* and tradition. He notes, however, that the *Sunna,* which the Abbasids inherited from their predecessors, was based not so much on the sacred precedents of the Prophet and his first companions as on Umayyad administrative improvisation and regulation. From this he drew the inference that the Caliph was at liberty to exercise his own discretion as well as to establish and to codify his own rules and regulations.[22] Ibn al-Muqaffaʿ makes his meaning quite clear. Since existing practice is inconsistent, frequently contradictory and not based on authentic prophetic precedents, it is the Caliph's duty to standardize existing usage and to initiate where there is none. His decisions may be reviewed by successive Caliphs. Ibn al-Muqaffaʿ agrees with the traditionists that the Caliph cannot abrogate the major religious commandments and if he tries to do so he must be disobeyed. This is the meaning of the tradition that there is no obedience in sin. He does, however, possess supreme discretionary authority (*ra'y*) in a wide range of political, administrative, financial and military matters. In general, says Ibn al-Muqaffaʿ, authority is discretionary (*al-ḥukm bi'l-ra'y*) in matters where there is no binding precedent (*athar*).[23]

Writing a little letter, al-Jāḥiẓ still seems to use the word *siyāsa* in the general sense of statecraft.[24] The same meaning is implicit in a dictum attributed to Ibn al-Furāt, who became Vizier in Baghdad in the year A.D. 909 and is cited as saying: "The basis of government is trickery. If it succeeds and endures, it becomes policy."[25]

At first, *siyāsa* is regarded as something distinct from religion but not contrasted with it. A saying attributed to Mu'āwiya speaks of "one who rules people by religion and worldliness" (*man yasūs al-nās bi'l-dīn wa'l-dunyā*), an old Persian dictum.[26] Similarly, Ibn al-Muqaffa' sees the religious and political functions of the Caliph as complementary rather than contradictory or contrasting. Even for al-Jāḥiẓ, who in so many ways represents an Arab reaction against Persianism, the difference is still basically one of place. *Siyāsa* is concerned with this world, religion with the other, and the same rules apply to both. "If this were not so," he says, "no kingdom could arise, no state be stabilized, no policy stand up."[27]

Some indication of the new connotation of *siyāsa* can be obtained from the terms with which it is frequently collocated in Arabic prose.[28] Linked with *tadbīr,* as often happens, it clearly connotes conducting the business of government; with *mulk*, the exercise of sovereignty. It may be good or bad—thus a tenth-century text speaks of the Byzantines as "governing (*yasūsūna*) their subjects oppressively (*bi-siyāsat jawr*)."[29]

From these and other texts it is reasonable to infer that the word *siyāsa* was coming, more and more, to mean the discretionary power exercised by the sovereign—any sovereign—and his officers as distinct from the authority conferred upon the Muslim Caliph by the holy law. The point is clarified in a very interesting passage written by the tenth-century author Abū Ḥayyān al-Tawḥīdī, recording a conversation which he had with the vizier. The vizier quotes the well-known platonic dictum that the world goes best when kings philosophize or philosophers reign. This, remarks the king, is not a sound principle since philosophy only befits those who renounce the world and devote themselves to the other world, which a king cannot do since he has to govern the people of this world (*wa huwa muḥtāj ilā siyāsati ahlihā*). Abū Ḥayyān replies that religion and government (*dīn* and *siyāsa*) are complementary, each requiring the other. *Sharī'a* he says, is the goverment of mankind by God; kingship is the government of mankind by man. *Sharī'a* without *siyāsa* is deficient; *siyāsa* devoid of *Sharī'a* is also deficient.[30]

Although the formulation is new, the idea is not, and there are many dicta, sometimes appearing as *ḥadīth,* sometimes as sayings attributed to the ancient Persians, that religion and power are twins and that neither can survive without the other. Abū Ḥayyān argues this logically and carries the argument an important step further. Significantly, this discussion dates from a period when we see the emergence of separate powers in Islam, both claiming religious sanction and authority, but the one more concerned with political and military affairs, the other confined to more strictly religious matters.

At about the same time we also find the word *siyāsa* being used quite frequently in a somewhat different sense, namely political philosophy. Beginning as statecraft with a connotation derived from Persian practice rather than Hellenistic thought, it becomes more theoretical and more theoretical and more philosophical and occurs in translations and adaptations of Greek writing, as for example in the translation of the alleged *Mirror of Princes* said to have been written by Aristotle for Alexander and known in Arabic as the *Kitāb al-siyāsa fī tadbīr al-ri'āsa.* This is, of course, still statecraft rather than philosophy. It has, however, acquired a clearly philosophical meaning when we come to the philosopher al-Fārābī, who indeed defines it in the fifth chapter of his *Classification of the Sciences*. This sense of the word, political philosophy, becomes one of the standard meanings of *siyāsa,* and is used by many writers subsequent to al-Fārābī, notably those who represent the Hellenistic tradition in Islamic thought.[31] At the same time, however, the earlier meaning of statecraft persists, as for example in the classical Persian work of Niẓām al-Mulk, known as *Siyāsatnāma,* usually translated as the *Book of Politics* or the *Book of Statecraft*.

But did *siyāsa* necessarily mean politics or statecraft at that time? Some enlightenment may be obtained by considering another text, the famous Arabic historical book *al-Fakhrī,* written in Mosul in the year 1302 by Ibn al-Tiqtaqā, in which he says: "*Siyāsa* is the chief resource of the king on which he relies to prevent bloodshed, defend chastity, prevent evil, subjugate evildoers and forestall misdeeds which lead to sedition and disturbance."[32] A great deal, at different times, has been expected from politics or statecraft or even political philosophy, but this seems a somewhat surprising list of anticipated results from the exercise of *siyāsa,* in whichever of these meanings the word is understood. The translations of *al-Fakhrī,* in both English and French, render *siyāsa* as politics. It does not, however, mean politics, and we may obtain a better understanding of what the term *siyāsa* meant to Ibn al-Tiqtaqā in Mosul in A.D. 1302, as well as to others of his time, if we look at some earlier texts.

A first clue may be found in a mid-tenth century work, the *Faraj ba'd al-shidda* of Tanūkhī. The passage, translated by Beeston, enumerates five sorts of civil servants, including "the one in the police department, who needs to be familiar with the rules of retaliation, the quranically prescribed penalties, matters of wounding and assault, and police court cases."[33] The final phrase, in the original, is *siyāsāt,* and Beeston's translation, assigning a penal meaning to the word, is clearly justified by the list of terms which precedes it.

There is no lack of supporting evidence. The Persian author Rāwandī notes that the king needs a chamberlain to administer punishment (*siyāsat afzāyad*).[34] In another Persian text, the *Qābūsnāma,* the writer advises those who would rule: "*bā siyāsat bāsh,*" which Levy translates "maintain a stern discipline."[35] The penal connotation of the term *siyāsa* is clear in another tenth-century work, the *Aḥkām sulṭāniyya* of al-Māwardī.[36] Al-Māwardī, as one would expect from a jurist, tries to give even to penal *siyāsa* a religious meaning. Other writers are less particular and a passage in a thirteenth-century Syrian text is especially revealing. The Damascene chronicler, Abū Shāma, speaking of the famous Zangid Prince Nūr al-Dīn, lays great stress on his piety. Among other indications of his devoutness and commitment to Islam, Abū Shāma makes a point of saying several times that Nūr al-Dīn returned to the *sharī'a,* abandoned the practice of *siyāsa, (wakāna la yu'mal bi'l-siyāsa,)* and abolished the office of *shiḥna,* a kind of police chief. Nūr al-Dīn's amirs then came to him, says Abū Shāma, and complained that lawlessness had become rife and that execution was needed to restore order. Adequate law enforcement, said the amirs, was impossible without *siyāsa.* Nūr al-Dīn, says Abū Shāma, refused and said: "We have no need of *siyāsa; Sharī'a* is sufficient."[37] In a second passage in Abū Shāma, the term *siyāsa* is used of the crucifixion of pro-Fatimid conspirators.[38]

From these and others texts it is clear that *siyāsa* here means neither politics nor statecraft but punishment. More particularly, it means punishment which is severe, physical, probably capital, and—this is the important point—not provided for by the *Sharī'a. Sharī'a* punishments—that is to say, the penalties laid down in the *Sharī'a* for offenses defined in the *Sharī'a,* are normally called *ḥadd. Siyāsa* is a punishment not prescribed by the *Sharī'a* for an offense not defined by the *Sharī'a.* It is punishment administered under the discretionary power of the ruler, for an offense against the authority of the ruler. In this sense it invariably means severe physical punishment and frequently death.

This comes to be the common meaning of *siyāsa* (*siyāsat*) in both Persian and Turkish, for many centuries. The word still occurs with the earlier meaning in Persian and Turkish,[39] as well as in Arabic, and is used in a theoretical sense, more particularly for the powers of the sovereign deriving from his discretionary royal authority as distinct from those powers conferred upon him as sovereign by the *Sharī'a.* In practice, however, it normally means the punishment inflicted by such authority, rather than the authority itself. *Siyāsatgāh,* in Persian and Turkish, does not mean a place of politics or government; it means a place where capital punishment is inflicted—a place of torture or execution. In this sense of discretionary punishment, the passage quoted above from the *Fakhrī* makes better sense, and the expected results not unreasonable.

The same point concerning the right of the sovereign to exercise discretionary powers is made by no less a person than Ibn Khaldūn who cites the precedent of the Umayyad and Abbasid Caliphs to demonstrate the right of the ruler to make laws.

By Mamluk times, the distinction between *Sharī'a* on the one hand and the commands and penalties known as *siyāsa* on the other led to a curious explanation of the latter term. In a number of different texts we find the argument put forward that the word *siyāsa* in fact has nothing to do with the Arabic verb *sāsa/yasūsu* or with the earlier meaning of politics, policy or statecraft. It is, according to this explanation, not of Arabic origin at all but is a mixture of Persian and Turkish or Mongol. *Sī* in Persian means 30; *yasa*, a Turko-Mongol word meaning prohibition and hence law or rule is the term commonly applied to the Mongol code of laws attributed to Jenghiz Khan.[40]

Maqrīzī, writing in the early fifteenth century, explicitly defines the distinction between *Sharī'a* and *siyāsa* jurisdictions, and gives the Mongol explanation of the latter term. In Egypt and Turkey, he says, since the coming of the Turks (meaning the Mamluks), rulers have recognized two kinds of judicial decision, *Sharī'a* and *siyāsa.* For the latter there were indeed in the Mamluk Sultanate separate courts and separate judges administering different systems of law. The explanation of a Mongol origin, although no doubt wrong etymologically, has some value as illustrating the course of events after the establishment of the regimes of the steppe peoples. Not surprisingly, there was a strong Islamic reaction against this situation, of which the ulema strongly disapproved.

That such a theory could be advanced at all indicates the degree to which the Muslim authors were aware of this distinction between sharīʿa justice and another kind of jurisdiction which, according to strict *Sharīʿa* concepts, should not have been admitted at all. It was this no doubt which led to the attempted compromise of Ibn Taymiyya and some other jurists who advanced a doctrine of *siyāsa sharʿiyya, siyāsa* according to the *Sharīʿa,* which was developed more particularly by his disciple Ibn Qayyim al-Jawziyya and revived and elaborated in modern times by the Wahhābīs and by the Salafiyya.[41]

In the Arabic-speaking countries the older meaning of *siyāsa* never died out. Ibn Khaldūn for example speaks of *siyāsa ʿaqliyya* and *siyāsa madaniyya,*[42] while some Maliki jurists use the expression *siyāsa ʿāmma* to include matters such as the division of the booty, the defense of the frontiers, and breaches of internal peace, which are excluded from the normal jurisdiction of the qadi.[43]

In the course of the nineteenth century, the term *siyāsa* along with a good deal of the Arabic vocabulary, underwent a process of neoclassical modernization. It acquired a somewhat Westernized sense which at the same time took it back to earlier classical Arabic usage. Sheikh Rifāʿa al-Ṭahṭāwī, the great Egyptian modernist, uses the term in his Arabic translation of the French constitution of 1830, to render such French words as *loi* and *reglement.*[44] The choice is significant. Arabic has after all a very considerable judicial vocabulary, and the fact that a scholar trained at al-Azhar felt that these Islamic legal terms were inappropriate for French words and used *siyāsāt* for laws and rules and regulations shows how the term was understood in his time.

In modern—i.e. late nineteenth and early twentieth-century Arabic—*siyāsa* and *siyāsī* mean exclusively, politics, policy and political in a more or less European sense, and much the same has happened in other Islamic languages which use the word. In modern Arabic the term is also occasionally used in the sense of diplomatic.

In Ottoman usage, *siyaset* is used almost exclusively in the sense of physical punishment for offenses against the State. The first formal statement on the subject occurs in the *kanunname* of Sultan Mehmed II dealing with offenses punishable by flogging and fines. It was later amplified by additional material contained in a *siyasetname,* prescribing capital or severe physical punishment (*siyaset*) for certain specified offenses, and laying down procedures.[45] The same term occurs in a number of later *kanunnames* and other legal documents. The common phrase in Ottoman chronicles that this or that offending minister was put to death *siyasaten* does not mean that he was executed politically but that the death sentence was imposed by the discretionary authority of the Sultan and not in fulfillment of a *ḥadd* for an offense against the holy law. The phrase *siyaseten katl,* or simply *siyaset,* is used commonly for the torture and/or execution of officials and other persons at the behest of the Sultan or even of other authorities. Thus, in a vivid passage, the historian Naima describes the dreadful tortures inflicted by French mercenaries, in the Sultan's service, on Russian and Cossack prisoners and uses the term *siyaset* to describe these acts.[46] Something of the older meaning seems to have lingered on however, as for example in a fifteenth-century Turkish couplet: "If kingship does not stand there will be no justice (*adalet*)/ If the word is not kept there will be no *siyaset.*"[47]

Most commonly, however, the word is used exclusively in the sense of physical punishment or even occasionally of torture. Even an early nineteenth-century historian like Jevdet, describing the events of 1821, uses the term *siyaset-i örfiye* for summary executions.[48] In the course of the nineteenth century, however, *siyaset* begins to acquire the meaning of politics, replacing the term *politika* favored by early nineteenth-century Ottoman historians. By the mid-century, Ottoman liberals are beginning to demand *hukuk-u siyasiye,* political rights, and from then on the older meaning rapidly disappears. In modern Turkish, as in modern Arabic, the word is used exclusively in the sense of policy and politics.

Chapter Five

Usurpers and Tyrants: Notes on Some Islamic Political Terms

Usurpers and Tyrants: Notes on Some Islamic Political Terms

The *Sharī'a*, the holy law of Islam, posits a divinely ordained community, the *umma*, ruled by a divinely ordained sovereign, the *imām*. To comply with the law, the *imām* must meet certain requirements:

1. He must be qualified, that is to say he must be one of a group of people possessing certain necessary minimal qualifications. These are differently defined by Sunnī, Shī'ite and Khārijite Muslims, but all agree that there are qualifications and that the *imām* must meet them.
2. He must become *imām* by a legally recognized and approved procedure. Here again there is a difference between the Sunnis and the Shī'a, the first prescribing election, the second hereditary succession within the House of the Prophet. Both of them however, and even the Khārijites, agree that succession must be in accordance with the holy law as defined and interpreted by them.
3. He must govern justly.

Granted the existence and acceptance of these rules, it follows that any ruler who fails to meet either the first or second requirement is not legitimate, i.e., is a usurper; any who violates the third is unjust, i.e., a tyrant. These categories may, but do not necessarily, coincide.

The different schools agree that obedience to the *imām* is a religious obligation, prescribed by holy law. From this it follows that disobedience is a sin as well as a crime. But in principle such obedience is owed only to a legitimate and just ruler. It may be withheld from an illegitimate or unjust ruler. Some go even further and argue that in such a case the duty of obedience not only lapses but is replaced by a right or rather duty of disobedience.

From the beginning, Islamic history, tradition and law embrace two distinct and indeed contradictory principles, one activist, the other quietist.[1] The advent of Islam was in itself a revolutionary challenge to the old leadership and the old order, both of which were overthrown and supplanted, the one by the Prophet and his companions, the other by Islam. This radical tradition was continued with what later historians have usually called conquests but what the Muslim tradition calls *futūḥ*, literally openings. These were seen not as conquests in the vulgar sense of territorial acquisitions, but as the overthrow of impious regimes and illegitimate hierarchies and the opening of their people to the new revelation and dispensation. The notion of the superseded old order is vividly expressed in the invocation of an ultimatum said to have been sent by the Muslim commander Khālid ibn al-Walīd to the princes of Persia: "Praise be to God who has dissolved your order (*ḥalla niẓāmakum*), frustrated your evil designs, and sundered your unity."[2] The use of the root *fataḥ* is thus not unlike the twentieth century use of the verb "liberate," and is indeed sometimes replaced by the latter verb (*ḥarrar*) in modern Arabic writing. The Arabic verb *ghalab*, conquer, with a connotation of triumph is sometimes used of the Muslim conquests, in the context of actual military operations. It is normally used of the conquest or reconquest of Muslim lands by the non-Muslim armies.

This underlying concept of the essential rightfulness of the Muslim advance tallies with the doctrine, expressed in a well-known *ḥadīth*, that every infant has an inborn predisposition to be a Muslim, but his parents make him a Jew or a Christian or a Zoroastrian. It is thus an opening, or a liberation, to give free vent to this divinely ordained propensity.[3] This spirit of activism is expressed many times in Islamic literature, notably in Qur'ānic injunctions not to obey wilful and intemperate rulers who bring corruption to the world, or in the traditions to the effect that there is no obedience in sin—i.e., that the duty of obedience lapses when the orders of the sovereign conflict with God's commandments.[4] If the first clearly refers to non-Muslim rulers, the second would seem to be directed against erring Muslim holders of authority.

The quietist tradition is also firmly based in the same Qur'ānic and traditional sources. The verse "Obey God, obey His Prophet and obey those in authority over you" is supported by numerous *ḥadīths*[5] enjoining the duty of obedience to legitimate authority, and was reinforced by the authoritarian traditions of the older societies which had flourished in the Middle East and became the political and cultural centers of the House of Islam.

In the course of the early Islamic centuries, there were significant changes in the definitions of legitimacy and justice and consequently in the definitions of usurpation and tyranny. The first and second requirements—legitimacy in terms of qualifications and manner of accession—were progressively reduced to the point when in effect only two conditions remained—power and Islam. As long as the ruler possessed the necessary authority to seize and hold power and as long as he was a Muslim, however minimal and however nominal, that sufficed.[6] Some were even willing to go a step further and admit the rule of a non-Muslim, but this was exceptional and in classical times was not generally admitted. The other qualification, that of ruling justly, was also whittled down though never finally eliminated. It was in fact reduced to one basic requirement—the public, though not necessarily the private, recognition and enforcement of the social and ritual prescriptions of the *Sharīʿa*.

In time the concepts of usurper and tyrant, previously distinct, begin to overlap and even coincide. Muslim writers on the related subjects of religion, law and history developed a rich vocabulary of technical terms to denote different kinds of rule and ruler. The evolution and specialization of the terms applied to rulers not recognized and, so to speak, not validated by the holy law help to document the history of political institutions and ideas.

The prototype of the non-*Sharīʿa* ruler is of course the infidel, particularly—but not exclusively—when he oppresses the apostles of God and their faithful. Such were Pharaoh, Haman, and other figures portrayed in the Qur'ān; such too were the pagan chiefs and rulers whom the Prophet Muḥammad ousted or converted in Arabia. The Christian kings whom the Muslims encountered outside Arabia, being followers of a revealed religion, have a somewhat better status, and are referred to by neutral or even respectful terms (*Ṣāḥib*, *'Aẓīm*) or by their own titles (*Najāshī*, *Qayṣar*). The term most commonly applied to non-Muslim rulers, whether before Muḥammad or outside the world of Islam, is *malik*, king, a term already sufficiently negative in its connotation in early Islam to be suitable for this purpose.

Later, when the title *malik* acquired a certain legitimacy within the Islamic world through its adoption by a succession of Muslim rulers, the practice grew of using other, less flattering terms for infidels. Some of these terms were also used for Muslim rulers who were seen as failing to meet the requirements.

One sometimes used was *ṭāghiya*, from a root frequently used in the Qur'ān both of rulers and of peoples. It carries a connotation of insolence and overweening pride, of disregard for God's law and hostility to His apostles—in a word, a kind of Muslim equivalent of the Greek notion of *hubris*. In the Qur'ān it is used of Pharaoh and other pagans who defied the will of God and were duly punished. In Islamic times it remained in use for rulers whose title to authority was not recognized. Thus, the 'Alid Muḥammad al-Nafs al-Zakiyya, in a *khutba* delivered in Medīna in 145/762, applied it to his successful rival the 'Abbāsid Caliph al-Manṣūr, whom he denounced as *hādhā al-ṭāghiya 'aduww Allāh*—"this tyrant the enemy of God."[8] It was used by Shī'a of Sunnī government[9] and by many Muslim writers of the Byzantine Emperors. Later, it was applied in North Africa to the Christian kings of Europe, while eastern writers continued to use the term *malik* for this purpose.

The rulers of the Christian states established by the Crusaders in Muslim territory do not qualify even for this title. They are not *malik*, king, but *mutamallik*, pseudo-king. Kings who came from Europe were called *malik*, e.g., Richard Coeur de Lion, Malik al-Inkitār, but the King of Cyprus, as Qalqashandī explains, was called *mutamallik* "because the Muslims had taken (*fataḥ*) Cyprus and then the Christians had conquered (*taghallab*) the island and ruled it. That is why the one who prevails over it is called *mutamallik* and is not called *malik*." The same title was used, for the same reason, of the Armenian king of Sīs and the Georgian king of Tiflīs, both cities conquered by the Muslims and then recaptured by the Christians.[10]

In principle, even a Muslim ruler who does not possess the necessary qualifications of descent and capacity or is not chosen or appointed according to the law, is a usurper. Among the Shī'a this remained a crucial question, and all Sunnī rulers, not being of the line of 'Alī and not being nominated and appointed by an 'Alid predecessor, are usurpers. Among Sunnī Muslims, as has been already noted, effective power became a sufficient qualification. In a phrase used by Mālikī jurists, *man ishtaddat waṭ'atuhu wajabat ṭā'atuhu*—"whose power prevails must be obeyed."[11] The ruler need no longer be of the tribe of Quraysh, nor even an Arab. He need no longer possess the legally prescribed qualifications of rectitude, judgment, physical soundness, wisdom and courage. It is sufficient if he can stay in power and keep order. The Khārijites, the Mu'tazila and a minority among Sunnī jurists go a little further, and demand that the ruler be guilty neither of blameful innovation (*bid'a*) nor of major sin (*fisq*). According to Baqillānī, for example, the *imām* forfeits his imāmate if he falls into this category and thus ceases to be legally qualified.

The same applies if he becomes senile or otherwise physically incompetent.[12] The majority Sunnī view was that the imām, even if he is a sinner (*fāsiq*), must be obeyed, though some authorities conceded that this might not apply to the *imām's* agents who are *fasaqa*.

In general, such limitations are either explicitly dropped or tacitly abandoned. Only one requirement survives the rest—that he rule justly. The notion of usurper has thus lost its meaning; that of tyrant remains. In other words, when a ruler is challenged on religious grounds, the challenge is based not on the manner in which he gained power but on the manner in which he exercises it—not usurpation, but tyranny.

Tyranny—it is generally agreed—is a great evil. But it is not the greatest evil. The dictum that "Tyranny is better than strife" is cited to defend a doctrine of quietism, of submission even to an evildoing and tyrannical authority, if the alternative is the collapse of all authority, and a situation in which the unity of the Islamic community would be disrupted and the legally valid execution of normal legal acts such as court judgments, the contracting of marriages, the division of inheritances, would cease to be possible.[13]

Anarchy was not the only alternative which was worse than tyranny. Another, according to some jurists, was the rule of an infidel monarch over Muslims. The advance of the Christian reconquest in Sicily and Spain gave this question a growing urgency. While some jurists were willing to concede a certain legitimacy to a Christian ruler who permitted his Muslim subjects to live according Muslim law, others took the opposite view, and insisted that if a Muslim country falls under infidel rule, its Muslim inhabitants must follow the scriptural precedent of the

Prophet and leave their homes, to migrate to a Muslim land. In a famous *fatwā* on the question whether Muslims might remain in Christian Spain, the Moroccan jurist al-Wansharīsī insists that they must leave, even if the new Christian regime is tolerant and just, and the Muslim regime to which they go is neither. A tolerant infidel is a greater threat to their faith, and therefore even Muslim tyranny is better than Christian justice.[14]

The terms used for tyranny, their synonyms and their antonyms, give some indication of how tyranny was perceived and defined. The commonest term is *ẓulm*, which occurs very frequently in the Qur'ān, where it appears to have the broad, general meaning of misdeed, wrongdoing, and hence injustice and tyranny. In post-Qur'ānic usage it is increasingly specialized in the latter sense, and is sometimes coupled with *jawr*, a word the primary meaning of which is deviation, straying from the path, whence also the developed meaning of wrongful or unjust treatment. One of the most commonly cited messianic traditions speaks of a *mahdī*, a divinely guided one, who will come and "fill the earth with *'adl* and *qisṭ* as it is now filled with *ẓulm* and *jawr*."[15] *'Adl* and *qisṭ*, usually translated justice and equity, express the converse of tyranny. The basic meaning of *ẓulm* is the absence of *ᶜadl*, and its political content changes as does that of *ᶜadl*.

Another word occurring frequently in the Qur'ān, with the meaning of an insolent and overbearing figure, is *jabbār*, sometimes coupled with *mutakabbir* (arrogant, self-important), *'anīd* (willful), *shaqī* (fractious) and *'āṣī* (rebellious, sinful). It is the converse of *taqī* (God-fearing) and *barr* (pious), and is no doubt related to the Hebrew *gibbōr*, which however has a positive and not a negative connotation. *Jabbār*, in the plural form *jabābira*, appears in a famous *ḥadīth* enumerating the stages of deterioration in the Islamic institution of sovereignty: "The Prophet said: After me there will be caliphs, and after the caliphs amīrs, and after the amīrs kings, and after the kings oppressors (*jabābira*), and then a man of my family will arise who will fill the world with justice (*'adl*) as it is now filled with tyranny (*ẓulm*)."[16] The *jabābira* obviously represent the final stage of wickedness, before the advent of the messianic age.

In general, the term *jabbār* is not much used in Islamic political literature, possibly because of its adoption as one of the divine names. Two other terms however gained some currency to denote oppressive or unauthorized rule.

The first is *istibdād*, which may be translated colloquially as doing it alone. As used in medieval texts, it carries a connotation of arbitrary and capricious rather than tyrannical or illegitimate rule. It is used of a ruler who decides and acts on his own, without due consultation of his religious and other advisors, and it is contrasted with *naṣīḥa* or *mushāwara*, as *ẓulm* is contrasted with *'adl*.[17] In the nineteenth and twentieth centuries *istibdād* came to be the term commonly used by liberal democrats, in both Turkish and Arabic, to characterize the autocratic rulers whom they wished either to limit or to remove.

In modern Arabic *za'īm* means leader, especially political leader. It was used as a military title in Mamlūk Egypt, and seems to have first come into use in the modern sense in the nineteenth century. It has usually been a positive term, which political leaders were happy to adopt. It was not always so. One of the meanings of the root is pretence or false claim, and the term *za'īm* was sometimes used in medieval Islamic documents for leaders or rulers whose title was for one reason or another invalid or at least unrecognized. It was thus used of the chiefs of the Ismā'īlīs in Persia and Syria, of the head of the Jewish community in Baghdad, and of certain Muslim rulers, such as the Zaydīs in the Yemen and the Almohads in North Africa, who claimed to be caliphs and whose claim was not admitted.[18] The modern expression *maz'ūm*, so-called, pretended, *soi-disant*, retains this connotation.

Ottoman usage retained the classical Islamic terminology, with some variants. Thus Christian kings were not called *malik* but *kiral*, a word of European origin. The Ottomans were very reluctant to apply any Islamic title, even those of Persian or Turkish origin, to non-Muslims, and only conceded this under pressure. The preferred term was *kıral* (feminine *kıralıçe*), sometimes followed, in accordance with a common Ottoman practice, by an abusive jingle—*kıral bedfi'āl*—evildoing king.

In modern Arabic most of these Qur'ānic and other classical terms can still be used, but have become somewhat archaic. Some others have taken their place. *Ghāsib*, which in classical usage usually refers to the forcible and illegal seizure or misappropriation of property, is given the political meaning of usurper. Among many synonyms for repressive or oppressive government, *iḍtihād*, is probably the most common. A loan word of European origin, *diktātūr* and *diktatūrī*, is also widely used of regimes in other countries.

Chapter Six

On the Quietist and Activist Traditions in Islamic Political Writing

On the Quietist and Activist Traditions in Islamic Political Writing

From the earliest times, the political tradition of Islam, on the one hand as formulated in Islamic theology and law, on the other hand as expressed in the accepted versions of early Islamic history, contains two distinct and in some measure even contradictory principles concerning the problems of government and obedience, of which one might be described as authoritarian and quietist, the other as radical and activist. The exponents of both these principles point to the authority of the Qur'ān and tradition, and to the example of the Prophet himself. Both principles are indeed exemplified in the career and teachings of the Prophet and in the history of the early caliphate, which constitute the shared memory and common heritage of Muslims everywhere. These two traditions may be examined separately.

Exponents of authoritarian principles frequently cite the Qur'ānic verse (4: 59) "Obey God, obey His Prophet and obey those in authority over you." In support of the meaning which they find in this verse, the defenders of authoritarian politics quote numerous *ḥadīths*, the general purport of which is that the subject owes unquestioning and immediate obedience to the legitimate authority—that is, to the lawful head of the *umma,* the Islamic religio-political community. Since the head of the *umma* has the right to appoint persons to act in his name, the duty of obedience also extends to those officers and officials who exercise properly delegated authority on behalf of the duly constituted sovereign. In earlier times, there was considerable insistence on the need for legitimacy and legality—the legitimacy of the sovereign himself, and the legal status of those claiming to exercise authority derived from him. With the passage of time, the question of legitimate accession seems to have lost its importance, and the attention of the jurists was shifted from the manner in which authority was acquired to the manner in which it was exercised. The hard lessons of a time of upheaval brought what was in effect a new principle—that any authority, however acquired, was legally valid as long as it preserved a basic minimum of legality, i.e., of respect for Islamic legal norms. Even this second principle, of legality rather than legitimacy as constituting a claim to obedience, was steadily whittled down, until it amounted to little more than the public acceptance and maintenance of the major Islamic ritual and moral principles.

While the limits on the authoritarian power of the sovereign were weakened, the duty of obedience on the part of the subject was correspondingly strengthened. Thus, the tenth-century Ḥanbalī jurist Ibn Baṭṭa (304/917–387/997) observed: "You must abstain and refrain from sedition. You must not rise in arms against the *imāms,* even if they be unjust. 'Umar ibn al-Khaṭṭāb, may God be pleased with him, said: 'if he oppress you, be patient; if he dispossess you, be patient.' The Prophet, may God bless and save him, said to Dharr: 'be patient, even if he be an Ethiopian slave'."[1]

The two quotations, the first ascribed to the Caliph 'Umar, the second to the Prophet himself, are almost certainly falsely attributed. Their purpose, however, is to justify doctrines expressed with increasing frequency in this period. One was to give unquestioning and unfaltering obedience to the sovereign power, however oppressive it might be; the other was to obey the agents of that power, however improbable the guise in which they appeared.[2]

Political writings of a literary and practical character are overwhelmingly on the side of the state—that is, for the rights of authority and the necessity of obedience. The one important exception to this is the early 'Abbāsid period, when spokesmen for the new regime still felt the need to justify their own successful revolution, but to do so with due care not to open the way for others. As the 'Abbāsid Caliphate acquired acceptance and legitimacy, writers on statecraft became more concerned with preserving, rather than challenging authority.[3] While they show keen awareness of the possibility of misrule by sovereigns and misgovernment by officials, they nevertheless usually insist that obedience must still be given, to avoid the greater evils of sedition and disorder. They suggest various ways in which rulers may be induced, by exhortation and good counsel, to govern justly, and are virtually unanimous on the need for honesty, loyalty and piety on the part of the officials whose function it is to administer the ruler's commands.

In the writings of the jurists and theologians, there is less willingness to relax the limits of authority or extend the limits of obedience, but even in this literature the political necessities of the time had their effect. The acceptance of this kind of quietism on the part of the jurists was not easy, and the terms in which it is expressed often indicate great anguish. These doctors of the holy law were men moved by profound religious conviction and deep moral purpose. Their acceptance of the need to submit to oppressive rule had its own character, entirely different from the flattery of the courtier, the pragmatism of the bureaucrat, or the submission of those who were afraid to express their doubts. Even oppressive government must be obeyed, they said, because the alternatives are worse, and because only in this way can the basic religious and legal prescriptions of Islam be maintained. In saying this, they made no pretence of liking or of respect for the oppressive government in question, nor did they make any attempt to conceal its oppressive character.

As early as the tenth century the point was made, very clearly, by Ibn Baṭṭa, the author already quoted:

> All the *'ulamā'* have agreed unanimously that the Friday prayers, the two festivals, the ceremonies of Minā and of 'Arafāt, warfare against the infidels, the pilgrimage, and the sacrifices are incumbent under every *amīr,* whether he be upright or an evildoer; that it is lawful to pay them the land tax, the legal alms, and the tithe; to pray in the cathedral mosques which they build and to walk on the bridges which they construct. Similarly, buying and selling and other kinds of trade, agriculture, and all crafts, in every period and under no matter what amīr, are lawful in conformity with the Book and the Sunna. The oppression of the oppressor and the

> tyranny of the tyrant do not harm a man who preserves his religion and adheres to the Sunna of his Prophet, provided that he himself acts in conformity with the Book and the Sunna, in the same way that if a man, under a just *imām,* makes a sale contrary to the Book and the Sunna, the justice of his *imām* will be of no avail to him. Similarly, it is lawful to resort to the jurisdiction of their judges, to secure the enforcement of legal punishments and penalties, to seek redress for wrongs from their *amīrs* or their police authorities, and to obey any officer whom they appoint . . . except in disobedience to Almighty God, for there is no duty of obedience to a creature (against his creator).[4]

In a passage which has been frequently quoted by modern scholars, Ibn Jamā'a, a Syrian jurist who flourished in the late thirteenth and early fourteenth centuries, is even more explicit:

> At a time when there is no *imām* and an unqualified person seeks the imāmate and compels the people by his power and his armies, without any *bay'a* or succession, then his *bay'a* is validly contracted and obedience to him is obligatory, so as to maintain the unity of the Muslims and preserve agreement among them. This is still so, even if he is barbarous or vicious, according to the best opinion. When the imāmate is thus contracted by force and violence to one, and then another arises who overcomes the first by his power and his armies, then the first is deposed and the second becomes *imām,* for the welfare of the Muslims and preservation of their unity, as we have stated.[5]

The desperation felt by an honest and pious observer of the political scene is clearly discernible in these lines.

Indeed, while the state as ideally conceived was a divinely ordained necessity for the benefit of the Muslims, the state as it existed in the world was often seen as a necessary evil, to be endured in order to avoid worse, but to be avoided as far as was possible. There is a line of thought, traceable in sayings attributed to some early figures, and worked out in detail by some later literary and religious writers, according to which government is inherently evil, and those engaged in it inevitably corrupted. "Paradise and government cannot be combined" runs an early saying, in striking anticipation of Lord Acton famous dictum that "power tends to corrupt and absolute power corrupts absolutely." An 'Abbāsid caliph in Baghdad is quoted as saying, when asked who is a happy man, "he doesn't know me and I don't know him." Even the acceptance of religious office under the state is sometimes condemned as a sacrifice of religious principle to worldly advantage, and the office of *qāḍī,* for example, an appointment made by the ruler, is often treated with contempt and ridicule in Islamic folklore. The refusal of the office of *qāḍī,* or of other government appointments, by theologians and jurists is a standard theme in pious biography, and an accepted indication of the piety and integrity of the subject.[6] The great theologian and philosopher al-Ghazālī is particularly eloquent and forceful on the oppressive and corrupt nature of government in his time and on the need for men of good faith to avoid contamination by it. Al-Ghazālī acted according to his own principles, when he withdrew first from teaching and then from public affairs, and made a vow not to attend any ruler's court, nor to accept any ruler's money. Later, under pressure, he emerged from retirement and accepted a teaching post.[7] Such views were widespread in times of political upheaval and oppression. They were, however, far from universal, and by the later Middle Ages an accord of sorts between the political and military authorities on the one hand and the men of religion and law on the other was usually achieved.

Among Sunnī Muslim jurists the principle came to be widely accepted that effective power was in itself a sufficient qualification. In a phrase sometimes used by jurists of the Mālikī school, *man ishtaddat waṭ'atuhu wajabat ṭā'atuhu*—"whose power prevails must be obeyed." Some lay down further requirements—that the ruler be guilty neither of blameworthy innovation (*bid'a*) nor of major sin (*fisq*). According to one view, if the ruler falls into either of these categories he ceases to be legally qualified and thus forfeits his right to rule.[8] The legal and practical implications of such a forfeiture, or of other grounds of forfeiture laid down by the jurists, such as the ruler becoming senile or otherwise physically incompetent, are not explored. Most Sunnī and many Shī'ite jurists, however, adhered to the view that the ruler, even if he be a sinner (*fāsiq*), must be obeyed as long as he respects the basic minimum, though some jurists conceded that while a sinful sovereign must be obeyed, the same privilege might not be extended to agents of the sovereign who are sinful.

Sinful rule and tyrannical government, it is agreed, are great evils, but in the authoritarian view they are not the greatest evils. Obedience must be given even to an evildoing and tyrannical ruler, if the alternative is chaos. Without authority, the unity of the Islamic community would be disrupted, the legally valid execution of normal legal acts such as court judgments, marriages, the division of inheritances, etc., would cease to be possible, and the most fundamental objective of government, to enable Muslims to live the good Muslim life, would no longer be met. If this should happen, the individual Muslim would lose that one thing which above all others it is the duty of the Muslim state to guarantee to him.

The *ḥadīth* quoted by Ibn Baṭṭa that "there is no duty of obedience to a creature against his creator" is clearly understood by him, in the context in which he quotes it, as referring to the irreducible minimum of religious commandments. There were some, however, both inside and outside the juristic schools, who interpreted these words, and other sayings of similar purport, in a wider and more specifically political sense.

While the predominant view among jurists supported the authoritarian tradition, increasingly reinforced by a doctrine of quietism, there was always another strand in the Islamic tradition, which one might call radical and activist—at times even revolutionary. This tradition is as old and as deep rooted as the other; its workings can be seen, through the centuries, both in Muslim political thought and in the political actions of Muslims.

Like the authoritarians, the exponents of the radical tradition looked to the life and teachings of the Prophet for guidance and inspiration. Both schools, in this context, concentrated their attention on the political actions which the Prophet found it necessary to undertake in order to accomplish his religious mission. But while the authoritarians looked to the Prophet as ruler, as head of a state, exercising sovereign authority over the community in Medina, the radicals looked rather to the earlier career of the Prophet when he was engaged in leading a movement of opposition to the pagan oligarchy of Mecca. Though this opposition was primarily religious and moral in purpose, it inevitably took the form of political action. In this perception, the Prophet began as a critic and opponent of the regime in Mecca, left his homeland for Medina, where he formed what in modern political parlance might be called a "government in exile," and from there was able to return to Mecca and accomplish the overthrow of the pagan regime and its replacement by a new Islamic order. In this as in so much else the Prophet was seen as a model, and his career as setting a pattern. Many later political aspirants attempted to follow his example; some of them succeeded, others failed. The 'Abbāsids who established themselves in the remote areas of eastern Iran, to build up their forces and ultimately return to Iraq; the Fāṭimids who went first to the Yemen and then to North Africa from which they came and conquered Egypt, were both in a sense trying to reproduce the prophetic sequence of opposition, struggle, migration, and advance from the periphery to the center. There have been many later leaders who tried to overthrow and supplant their rulers, by following the same route.

The activists, like the quietists, were also able to find texts in the Qur'ān which could be interpreted as justifying their position. The injunctions not to obey various ancient and pagan tyrants were obvious examples. Thus we read (XVIII: 28): "And keep thy soul content with those who call on their Lord morning and evening, seeking His Face; and let not thine eyes pass beyond them, seeking the pomp and glitter of this life; nor obey any whose heart we have permitted to neglect the remembrance of Us, one who follows his own desires, whose case has gone beyond all bounds." Another example (XXVI: 150–2): "But fear God and obey me and follow not the bidding of those who are extravagant, who make mischief in the land, and mend not [their ways]." The implication, that there is no duty of obedience to wrongdoing rulers, but on the contrary a duty of disobedience, is reinforced by numerous *ḥadīths* to the same effect.

During the first two centuries of Islamic history, there were two occasions in which the question of obedience and disobedience was posed in a paradigmatic form. The first occurred on 17 June 656, when the Caliph 'Uthmān was murdered. 'Uthmān, the third Caliph, was not the first to be murdered. But while his predecessor 'Umar was murdered by a disgruntled and probably demented Persian freedman, 'Uthmān was attacked and killed by Muslim Arab rebels. It was a profound and portentous difference, and was followed by the first of the series of divisive civil wars that split the Islamic state and community, and ultimately the Islamic religion. The perception of these wars and the arguments put forward on behalf of the participants are now better understood thanks to the discovery and study of some previously unknown sectarian sources.[9] In the course of the argument two basic positions emerged. According to the one, 'Uthmān was both a rightful and a just ruler, and his killing was therefore both a crime and a sin. According to the other, 'Uthmān was a wrongful and unjust ruler, and his killing was therefore an execution—a lawful, indeed a necessary act. For those who hold this view, it would be equally true whether 'Uthmān be condemned as a usurper, occupying a position to which he had no right, or as a tyrant, who erred not by his acquisition of power but rather by his manner of exercising it. The definition of the killing of the Caliph also determined the treatment to be accorded to the killers. If ʿUthmān was a just and rightful ruler, then those who killed him were rebels and murderers, and it was the duty of all good Muslims to assist in their apprehension and punishment. If ʿUthmān was a wrongful and unjust ruler, those who killed him had performed a good deed, and were entitled to the protection which in fact they received. Whatever the circumstances may have been at the time, in later perceptions the main charge against ʿUthmān—later extended to include his two predecessors—was usurpation rather than tyranny, and his crime was thus that he had occupied a position which rightfully belonged to another, namely, to ʿAlī, who was therefore justified in sheltering the killers of ʿUthmān and in refusing to surrender them to the vengeance of Muʿāwiya, ʿUthmān's kinsmen and himself, according to this view, a usurper. In time, after a long and complex evolution, these two viewpoints became associated, the one with Sunnī, the other with Shīʿite Islam. It would be an error simply to equate the Sunnīs with the quietist and the Shīʿa with the activist traditions. The Sunnīs, again and again, produced their own radicals and rebels; the Shīʿa evolved their own doctrines—and practice—of submission. Even the Imāms are quoted to this effect.[10] But broadly speaking, quietism has been more characteristic of Sunnī rejection of Shīʿī political thought.

The second occasion when the problem arose in an acute form, involving the whole Islamic world in a dispute concerning its rightful chief, was the sequence of events now commonly known as the ʿAbbāsid revolution. Here again, the discovery of new evidence, and a better understanding of old evidence, has thrown new light on the challenges and issues, the aspirations and the disappointments, that were involved in the overthrow of the Umayyads, the victory of the alliance of ʿAbbāsids and ʿAlids, and the defeat and elimination of the latter by the former.[11] Such documents as the writings of the *Daʿwa,* the speeches either delivered or put in the mouth of the early leaders, and the letters exchanged between the ʿAbbāsid Caliph Manṣūr and the Ḥasanid rebel Muḥammad ibn ʿAbdallāh, are key texts in the evolution both of the activist challenge and the quietist response.

Activist teachings were on occasion invoked in specific terms to justify disobedience to existing regimes, or their forcible overthrow. A number of medieval texts, particularly from the period of radical ferment in the eighth and ninth centuries, give some indication of what was perceived as bad government, calling for action against it. Thus Zayd ibn ʿAlī, who led a rebellion in 121/738, is quoted as follows:

> We summon you to the Book of God, to the Sunna of His Prophet, may God bless and save him, to wage Holy War against oppressors and defend those who have been abased, to give pay to those who are deprived of it and to share the booty equally among those who are entitled to it, to make good the wrongs done by the oppressors, to recall those who have been kept too long on campaigns, and to aid the House of the Prophet against those who obstruct us and disregard our rights.[12]

Another text, frequently repeated by medieval Arab authors, quotes the complaint of a disappointed revolutionary—one who had supported the ʿAbbāsid revolution against the Umayyads, in the hope of achieving better things, and was greatly dissatisfied with the results:

> By God, our booty, which was shared, has become a perquisite of the rich; our leadership, which was consultative, has become arbitrary; our succession, which was by the choice of the community, is now by inheritance. Pleasures and musical instruments are bought with the portion of the orphan and the widow. The *dhimmīs* lord it over the persons of the Muslims, and evildoers everywhere govern their affairs.[13]

In about 840, al-Jāḥiẓ, one of the greatest writers in Arabic literature, in the course of a lengthy discussion of tyranny and revolt, offers his own definition of bad government: "These [bad] rulers take ... hostages ... a friend for a friend, and a kinsman for a kinsman; they terrorize the good and encourage the wicked, and rule by favoritism and caprice, the flaunting of power, contempt for the people, repression of the subjects, and accusations without restraint or discretion."[14] In the essay from which these words are taken, al-Jāḥiẓ, defending the right to rule of the ʿAbbāsid caliphs, was confronting the eternal problem of successful revolutionaries—to justify their own actions in overthrowing their predecessors and seizing power, without at the same time giving anticipatory justification to others who might want to do the same to them.

The activists and quietists alike did not answer, or even ask, the crucial question which a modern constitutional lawyer would put: who is to determine, and by what procedures, whether a government has indeed become sinful, and therefore forfeited the right to govern. In fact, of course, the practical issue was decided time and again in the centuries of Islamic history by the arbitrament of political and where appropriate other forms of struggle.[15]

Chapter Seven

"Malik"

King

"Malik"
King

The tumult and the shouting dies;
The Captains and the Kings depart;
Still stands Thine ancient sacrifice,
An humble and a contrite heart.

Rudyard Kipling

In a verse attributed to the pre-Islamic Arabic poet 'Abīd ibn al-Abraṣ, he speaks of his tribe as *laqāḥ,* a word which, according to the ancient commentators and lexicographers, is applied to a tribe which has never submitted to a king. 'Abīd's verse makes the meaning clear:

> "They refused to be servants of kings, and were never ruled by any:
> When they were called on for help in war, they responded gladly."[1]

Both the ancient Arabs and the ancient Israelites, in their tribal phase, mistrusted kings and the institution of kingship. When the Israelites, dissatisfied with the administration of the Prophet Samuel's sons, came to him and asked "now make us a king to judge us like all the nations," Samuel was displeased, and God, it seems, shared his displeasure. "And Samuel told all the words of the Lord unto the people that asked of him a king." He warned them of what they might expect of a king—a descending spiral of taxation and conscription, confiscation, forced labor and servitude—"and ye shall cry out in that day because of your king which ye shall have chosen you; and the Lord will not hear you in that day." Nevertheless the Israelites persisted in their desire for a king, and had to endure the consequences, which the later prophets frequently pointed out to them (1 Samuel, Chapters 8 and 9).

The ancient Arabs, like the ancient Jews, were familiar with the institution of monarchy in the surrounding countries, and some were led to adopt it. There were kings in the states of Southern Arabia; there were kings in the border principalities of the north, in the realms of Ghassān and Ḥīra. All of these were in different degrees marginal to Arabia. The sedentary kingdoms of the south used a different language, and were part of a different culture, in many respects alien to Bedouin Arabia. The border principalities of the north, though authentically Arab, were deeply influenced by Persian and Byzantine imperial practice, and represent a somewhat alien element in the ancient Arab world. But even among the tribes, the royal title was not unknown. The earliest surviving inscription in the Arabic language, a funeral inscription of 328 AD found at Namāra, commemorates Imru'l-Qays ibn 'Amr, "King (*Malik*) of all the Arabs, who wore the diadem and subjugated Asad and Nizār and their kings." The epitaph ends with the claim that no king (*Malik*) until this time had attained what he had attained."[2] Namāra is in the Syrian borderlands, and the king commemorated in the epitaph seems to have been a member of the Lakhmid Dynasty, which ruled in the border principalities.

The pre-Islamic history of Bedouin Arabia is little known, and is encrusted with all kinds of myths and legends. The corporate memory preserves the recollection of one attempt to establish a monarchy—the short lived kingdom, indeed empire, of Kinda, which flourished in the late 5th and early 6th centuries. The realm of Kinda disintegrated, and the general attitude of the Arabians, sedentary as well as nomadic, was hostile to monarchy. Even in a town like Mecca, the Arabs preferred to be led by consensual chiefs, rather than commanded by monarchs.

This negative attitude towards monarchy is in general reflected in the Qur'ān and in the traditions. Mostly *Malik* occurs as one of the divine epitaphs, and as such is of course endowed with sanctity. When applied to human beings, it usually has an unfavorable connotation. Thus in Chapter XII of the Qur'ān, in narrating the story of Joseph, the word king *(Malik)* is commonly used of Pharaoh—hardly the model of a good and just ruler. In one passage (XVIII, 78/79) the Qur'ān speaks of a "king who confiscates every good ship," while in another (XXVII, 34) the Queen of Sheba, in conversation with Solomon, remarks that "when kings enter a city, they pillage it and make its nobles destitute. Thus do kings." It is noteworthy that David and Solomon, both very positive figures in the Qur'ān, though depicted in monarchical splendor, are not actually designated by the world *Malik*. The only one of the ancient Israelite kings expressly designated as such in the Qur'ān is the somewhat equivocal figure of Saul, in the Qur'ānic version called Ṭālūt, in a narrative which parallels the version in 1 Samuel VIII. (Qur'ān, II, 247/246 ff). In another passage (V, 23/20) the Qur'ān, reproaching the Jews of Medina with their ingratitude, reminds them of God's benefactions to them in the past—"He gave you prophets and made you kings, and gave you what He gave to no others in the world." Here again, the reference to kings, though not explicitly hostile, is less than favorable.

During the early Islamic centuries, it became customary to contrast kingship with caliphate. While the latter represented Islamic government under God's law, kingship was taken to mean arbitrary personal rule without this religious and legal basis. Ṭabarī tells of a conversation between the caliph 'Umar and the first Persian Muslim, Salmān:

"Salmān said that 'Umar said to him: "Am I a king or a caliph?" And Salmān answered: "If you have taxed the lands of the Muslims one dirham, or more or less, and applied it to unlawful purposes, then you are a king not a caliph." And 'Umar wept."[3]

A similar distinction is made by the historians of the 'Abbasid period, to separate the regime of the Umayyads from those of both their predecessors and successors. In their narratives, and even in their tables of contents, the historians speak of the "Caliphate" of the first four rulers of Islam, followed by the "kingdom" (*Mulk*) of Mu'āwiya and the other Umayyads, until the return of the Caliphate with the accession of the 'Abbasid dynasty. Only one of the Umayyads, 'Umar II, in recognition of his piety, is accorded the title of Caliph in subsequent historiography. All the rest are designated—perhaps more accurately denigrated—as kings, and their periods of rule as kingdom or kingship.

The point is made quite explicitly in the early 9th century by al-Jāḥiẓ, in a propaganda tract putting the 'Abbasid case against the Umayyads. Under the rule of the latter, he says, the Imamate became a Persian kingdom and the Caliphate a Byzantine usurpation, literally a Chosrean kingdom and a Caesarean usurpation.[4] Given this connotation of the title king, it is not surprising that it was used for the rulers of the infidels—for the Byzantine Emperor, the King of Nubia, and various monarchs of Christian Europe and others collectively known as *Mulūk al-Kuffār*, the kings of the unbelievers, or *Mulūk al-Kufr*, the kings of unbelief.

In early Islamic times the term king was thus commonly used to diminish others rather than to aggrandize oneself. There are however some signs of another attitude persisting, or perhaps recurring, in Islamic usage. Court poets and some other professional eulogists, seeking for fresh titles with which to glorify their patrons, sometimes had recourse to the word king. But this remained rare and entirely unofficial. It is not until the middle of the 10th century that we find the word *Malik* in official usage, occurring in inscriptions and coins, used by rulers to describe themselves. The first to adopt this title were the Samanids. They were followed by the Buyids, the Seljuqs, and the Ayyubids as well as other, lesser dynasties.

The significance of this return to royal style is clear. By this time the central authority of the Islamic empire had lost all effective control of the provinces, which were ruled by what began as hereditary governorships and in time became local dynasties. The use of the title *Malik* does not indicate a claim to equality with the caliph or, later, with the Sultan. It serves rather to assert a local sovereignty, under the loose suzerainty of a supreme imperial ruler elsewhere. In this it is roughly equivalent to the contemporary use of the title king by various monarchs in Europe, under the nominal supremacy of the Holy Roman Emperor.

The reason for the choice of this title, among the many possibilities offered by the rich lexical resources of the Arabic language, is not difficult to guess. The Samanids and their successors arose and ruled in lands of Iranian culture, where the monarchical traditions of ancient Iran were still very much alive. Iranian court style etiquette and even titulature had already affected the court of the ʻAbbasid Caliphs themselves. These influences were all the stronger in the capitals of the new states that were arising in the actual territory of Iran. The old Persian title Shāh was still too alien and too heathen to be adopted by Muslim rulers, but its Arabic equivalent, *Malik*, served in its place.

From the first, the title *Malik* was normally combined with an honorific adjective or participle, of the type used in the regnal title of the Caliphs themselves, but, in earlier times at least, avoiding those actually used as caliphal titles. The association was certainly intentional. On a coin struck in Bukhara in 349/960, the Samanid Prince ʻAbd al-Malik ibn Nūḥ is described as al-Malik al-Muwaffaq.[5] There was no caliph called al-Muwaffaq, though, perhaps coincidentally, that title had been used by a famous regent in Baghdad a century earlier. In a coin, also struck in Bukhara and dated 352/963, another Samanid Prince, Manṣūr ibn Nūḥ, used the title al-Malik al-Muẓaffar.[6] This again was a title of the Caliphal type, though not one that had actually been used by a Caliph. Later, as noted, the use of the title *Malik*, with or without accompanying adjective, became commonplace among Muslim dynasties.

While the use of *Malik* followed by an adjective became normal, it still remained rare in the construct form, i.e., followed by another noun or nouns indicating the territories or people over whom the "King" claimed to exercise his kingship. An interesting form is *Malik al-Mulūk,* King of Kings, an obvious echo of the ancient Persian Shāhanshāh.[7] This title is specifically condemned by early ḥadiths according to which the Prophet said that no man should call himself King of Kings since only God can be so described. According to a story told by Ibn al-Athīr,[8] the Sultan Jalāl al-Dawla asked the Caliph al-Qā'im that he be addressed as king of kings, but the Caliph refused this title as contrary to religion. According to the story the Sultan Jalāl al-Dawla then sought the opinion of the *Fuqahā'*. Abu'l-Ḥasan al-Māwardī opposed this, but other *Fuqahā'* approved it as lawful, and the Sultan therefore adopted this style. This new title is already attested at an earlier date. In an embroidery found in Iraq, it is applied to the Buyid prince Bahā' al-Dawla Abū Naṣr ibn 'Aḍud al-Dawla who died in 403/1012. It later makes an occasional appearance in the titulature of other Buyid and Ayyubid Princes, and according to literary sources, was occasionally used among the titles of the Mamluk Sultans of Egypt and as a form of address to the rulers of North Africa in Mamluk times.[9]

A few other compound titles using the term *Malik* occur. One such is *Malik al-Islām*, used of Sultan Maḥmūd of Ghaznī in an inscription in that city, dated 421/1030. It reappears in an inscription in Damascus, dated 475/1082–1083, and is used of the Seljuq Sultan

Alp Arslan in a letter of appointment in the name of his son Tutush. The title *Malik al-Umarā'* is said by Qalqashandī to have been used by the chief of the amirs at the Mamluk court.[10]

Titles with a territorial or ethnic content of a rather general nature occur in the titulature of the Mamluk Sultans of Egypt and later of the Ottoman Sultans. Such was *Malik al-barrayn wa'l-baḥrayn*, King of the Two Lands and the Two Seas. This seems to have been first used by an Ayyubid in an inscription on the Citadel of Boṣrā, dated 647/1249–1250, and thereafter became commonplace in both Mamluk and Ottoman usage.[11] For the Mamluks, the two seas appear to have been the Red Sea and the Mediterranean; for the Ottomans, the Mediterranean and the Black Sea. The title *Malik al-Qiblatayn* appears in an inscription of Baybars dated 664/1265–1266, in Kara. The two qiblas are presumably to Mecca and Jerusalem. Another rather general geographical title is *Malik al-Mashriq wa'l-Maghrib*, King of the East and the West, a title adopted in the 5th/11th century by some Seljuq rulers.[12]

Titles defining a territorial or national kingdom, such as are commonplace in ancient, medieval, and modern European titulature, are almost unknown. A few examples however occur. Such general titles as "King of the Arabs and Persians and Turks," used by some Mamluk and Ottoman rulers, are in effect claims to universal Islamic sovereignty, of the same type as those cited above, but a few local titles appear in inscriptions. In particular the pre-Ottoman Turkish rulers of Anatolia, no doubt influenced by current usage among the peoples whom they had recently conquered, sometimes struck coins or wrote inscriptions with territorial titles. Thus we find a king of the land of Rum and of Armenia, in an inscription in Bayburt of 610/1213–1214; a king of the land of Rum and Yunan, in an inscription in Ankara of 594/1197–1198; a king of Diyār Bakr in an inscription in Mayyāfāriqīn of 561/1165–1166. One or two similar titles appear claiming kingship over Egypt and Syria and Western Arabia, in late Ayyubid and early Mamluk titulature.[13]

Other titles used by the Buyids include *Malik al-Umam,* King of the Nations, and *Malik al-Dawla,* King of the State.[14]

In the period following the Mongol conquests, the petty sovereignties and autonomous Amirates that had characterized the Islamic Middle Ages disappeared, and most of the Islamic world was ruled by a small number of major states, the rulers of which used either the Arabic title Sultan or such Persian and Turco-Mongol titles as Shah, Padishah, Khan, Il-Khan, and the like. The title *Malik* survived principally in two contexts; as a component, of no special significance, in the string of titles and honorifics forming the style and titulature of the Ottoman and other Emperors, and as a designation for European and other infidel rulers. It was only in the latter context that the term denoted sovereignty and was used for a particular place and people. In Ottoman usage, European monarchs were usually designated by the title *kiral,* taken from Slavic or Hungarian; in Arabic, especially in North Africa, the relatively neutral term *Malik* was often replaced, in this context, by the condemnatory *ṭāghiya* and *ṭāghūt.*[15]

Malik reappears as a title in Islamic political usage in the 20th century, this time clearly as a reflection of Western and more particularly British usage. The first

Muslim ruler to use to title king (*Malik*) appears to have been the Sharīf Ḥusayn, who declared himself king of the Hijaz in 1916. He was followed by his son Fayṣal, who proclaimed an Arab Kingdom in Syria in 1920 and, after the failure of that adventure, became King of Iraq in 1921. In 1922 he was followed by the ruler of Egypt, where the ruling dynasty had changed their titles several times. Beginning as Ottoman Pashas, they had changed their titles successively to Khedive to declare their autonomy, and Sultan to declare their independence, as against the Ottomans. The title king—that used by the ruler of Britain himself—served to proclaim independence from Britain.

Others followed. The most important was Ibn Saud, who established the Saudi Arabia monarchy in 1926. Later in Morocco a switch from Sultan to king served the same purpose as it had in Egypt at an earlier date, namely that of declaring independence against a European suzerain power. Royal titles were similarly adopted at a later date in Jordan and Libya.

In more recent times the institution of monarchy, and with it the use of regnal titles, has been under attack from two sides—on the one hand by liberals and leftists of various persuasions, who have seen a republican form of government as more in accord with their ideologies and aspirations; on the other by Muslim fundamentalists, who have reverted to an earlier Islamic condemnation of hereditary and monarchical government.

Some monarchs still survive; others have been overthrown and replaced by republican regimes, most but not all of them of military origin. The captains and the kings now share the Islamic world, and neither show any inclination to depart.

Chapter Eight

The Regnal Titles of the First Abbasid Caliphs

The Regnal Titles of the First Abbasid Caliphs

The Abbasids, after coming to power, introduced many changes into the titulature and ceremonies of the Islamic Caliphate. One of the earliest of these was the practice whereby a member of the dynasty, on his accession as Caliph or designation as heir, adopted a special personal title or epithet, by which he was thereafter known.[1] From the eighth Caliph, *al-Mu'taṣim billāh,* onwards, these regnal titles are all in a standard form; though commonly abbreviated to the first word only, they consist of an adjectival phrase, qualifying the holder and formulating a relationship to God, with Whose name the formula ends—as for example *al-Mutawakkil ['alà 'llāh],* 'placing his reliance on God', *al-Musta'īn [billāh],* 'seeking for help from God', etc. The titles of the first eight Caliphs do not conform to this pattern, and show greater variation in both form and significance.

Many of the innovations of the Abbasids can be explained by reference to pre-Islamic practice, especially in Persia; others may be seen as developments from the usage of their Islamic predecessors. Neither of these methods of explanation throws any light on the distinctive Abbasid practice of personal regnal titles. No such titles were ever adopted by the patriarchal or Umayyad Caliphs, nor does the protocol of either the Sasanid or the Byzantine court offer any recognizable antecedents. We must, therefore, look elsewhere for the origins of this new practice, adopted so soon after the Abbasid accession to power.

Van Vloten, in his pioneer work on the origins of the Abbasid movement, drew attention to the importance of messianic beliefs as a motive force in this and other risings against the Umayyads, and showed how the Abbasids deliberately adapted some of their slogans and emblems in order to comply with the prophecies which were current at the time.[2] In medieval Islam as in medieval Christendom, the coming of a divinely guided leader who would overthrow tyranny and 'fill the world with justice'[3] was no vague dream of a remote future, but a firm and specific promise due for certain and imminent fulfilment. The prophecies which expressed and defined these expectations—the Sibylline and Johannine books in Christendom, the books of *jafr* and *malāḥim* in Islam, and the like[4]—were widely known, believed, and exploited, and for this reason often had a direct influence on political developments, affecting the attitudes of subjects, the claims of rulers, the appeals of leaders, and even the judgments of historians. "In almost every new monarch", says Professor Norman Cohn, speaking of medieval Europe, "his subjects tried to see that Last Emperor who was to preside over the Golden Age, while chroniclers bestowed on him the conventional messianic epithets, *rex justus* or maybe David. When each time experience brought the inevitable disillusionment people merely imagined the glorious consummation postponed to the next reign and, if they possibly could, regarded the reigning monarch as a 'precursor'.... And there was never any lack of monarchs to appeal, with varying degrees of sincerity or cynicism, to these persistent hopes."[5] Such appeals did not of course come only from monarchs; there were also many popular religious and other rebel leaders who presented themselves as the divinely appointed saviors foretold in the prophecies.[6] Such leaders usually took care to accommodate themselves to the signs and portents that heralded the coming of the messianic age, and adopted titles and epithets appropriate to their claims.

Islamic history offers many parallels to the millenarian movements in Christendom, so well described by Professor Cohn. The earliest attested messianic claims are those put forward by the followers of the rebel Mukhtār, in Umayyad times.[7] Thereafter there is a long line of messianic aspirants, continuing to the famous Mahdī of the Sudan and even, albeit in somewhat altered forms, to our own time.[8] One of the most famous of these movements in the Middle Ages was that which culminated in the establishment of the Fatimid Caliphate; it is significant that the Fatimids, despite their Ismāʿīlī faith and their bitterly anti-Abbasid attitude, followed the Abbasid practice of adopting regnal titles—and that the titles of the first two Caliphs were al-Mahdī and al-Qā'im,[9] both unmistakably messianic in purport.

What then of the Abbasids themselves, who originated the practice, and whose connection with messianic claims and apocalyptic expectations has been clearly demonstrated?[10] The titles of the third and fourth Caliphs, al-Mahdī and al-Hādī, are indeed of a familiar messianic pattern; the circumstances in which al-Mahdī was given this name, on his appointment as heir, are strongly suggestive of an appeal for popular support based on messianic expectations, as are some of his subsequent actions.[11] But if the use of such titles is part of an attempt by the Abbasids to present their advent as the fulfilment of messianic prophecies, one would expect this attempt to go back to the beginnings of the Abbasid mission, and not to make its appearance with the third reign. The first militant leader of the Abbasid house, Ibrāhīm b. Muḥammad … ibn al-'Abbās, the patron of Abū Salama and Abū Muslim, was indeed known to his followers as Ibrāhīm al-Imām. But he died before the advent of the dynasty, and his two brothers, who reigned as the first and second Abbasid Caliphs, are known to history by the regnal titles of al-Saffāḥ and al-Manṣūr. Neither of these, at first sight, fits into the religious and messianic pattern of such names as al-Imām and al-Mahdī, and their appearance between them suggests a surprising discontinuity of practice. The difficulty, however, is more apparent than real.

The title al-Saffāḥ can soon be set aside. This name, which has been variously explained as meaning 'the generous' and 'the bloodthirsty',[12] was almost certainly not used as regnal title by the Caliph himself; it was assigned to him by later historians, whose sense of order and propriety required that the first Abbasid, like all his successors, should have a regnal title of some sort.[13] The earlier historians, such as Jahshiyārī, Ṭabarī, Ya'qūbī and Dīnawarī, commonly refer to the first Abbasid Caliph by his *kunya* Abu'l-'Abbās; Mas'ūdī appears to have been the first to give him the regnal title of al-Saffāḥ, and he was followed in this by later historians.[14] The name al-Saffāḥ was probably taken from the Caliph's famous and frequently quoted address in Kufa in 132/750, in which he declares "*anā al-saffāḥ al-mubīḥ wa'l-thā'ir al-mubīr.*"[15] There may also have been some confusion, by historians, between the Caliph and his uncle 'Abdallah b. 'Alī, who, according to some sources, was known as al-Saffāḥ because of his brutal repression of the Umayyads in Syria.[16] The Caliph himself used no formal regnal title, but appears to have been given various epithets by his followers. Dīnawarī frequently refers to him as al-Imām;[17] Mas'ūdī says that he was first called al-Mahdī.[18] Hilāl al-Sābi', a well-informed authority on court matters, remarks that there was some uncertainty about his *laqab*, and that he was variously known as al-Qā'im, al-Muhtadī, and al-Murtaḍā, until the *laqab* al-Saffāḥ prevailed.[19] The religious and messianic character of these names is clear.

There remains the name of al-Manṣūr, the second and greatest of the Abbasid Caliphs, and in many ways the true founder of the Abbasid Empire. There is no doubt about his adoption and use of this name as a regnal title; the name itself, usually translated "the Victorious", seems to accord well with the imperial role that he played. Granted that the last of the Abbasid pretenders and the first of the Abbasid Caliphs used messianic titles, does not the long reign of al-Manṣūr constitute an inexplicable gap before the reappearance of messianic title with al-Mahdī and al-Hādī?

It does not. In the first place, the name al-Manṣūr does not, strictly, mean victorious. It is a passive participle, meaning 'the one who is aided [by God to win victory]', and is thus of the same pattern, both grammatically and theologically, as the familiar al-Mahdī—'the one who is guided [by God on the right path].' The use of the title al-Manṣūr with a messianic connotation is amply attested in the Arabic sources, and can be traced well back into pre-Abbasid times. Its significance is explained in an important passage in the *Shams al-'ulūm* of Nashwān al-Ḥimyarī (d. ca. 573/1117), the famous writer on the traditions and legends of Southern Arabia. Al-Manṣūr, he says, is an epithet (*laqab*) given to a messianic figure who is awaited (*qā'im muntaẓar*) by many people. This is the Mahdī, whom every group claims as one of their own. Thus for the Jews he is the Messiah of the house of David, for the Christians the son of Maryam, for the Sabi'ans a descendant of Hermes the Greek, for the Magians a descendant of Bahram Gur, who will restore the old Persian faith. The Shi'ites have a number of versions, each sect claiming that their *imām* is the Mahdī. The Ḥimyarites said, in their traditions taken from their learned men, that he was a man of Ḥimyar, a descendant of the Sabaeans on both sides, who would restore the kingdom to Ḥimyar with justice (*bi'l-adl*).[20] The same tradition is alluded to in another work from Southern Arabia, the *Iklīl* of Ibn al-Ḥā'ik al-Hamdānī (3rd–4th/9th–10th centuries), according to which Mount Dāmigh was said to have been the mountain of al-Manṣūr, that is, the Manṣūr of Ḥimyar.[21] Both these works are late, but refer to earlier material, including verses attributed to the Tubba' As'ad and recorded by 'Ubayd b. Sharya al-Jurhumī. Though these sources are obviously legendary, the traditions and sayings ascribed to them are very ancient. They depict the Manṣūr as a messianic figure, variously known as Manṣūr Ḥimyar, Manṣūr al-Yaman, and al-Qaḥṭānī, who would restore the lost glory of the South.[22]

With the help of these and similar passages in the literature of Southern Arabian legends and antiquities, it is possible to explain some otherwise puzzling allusions in the accounts, given by early historians, of revolts against the Umayyads. During the revolt of Mukhtār in Kufa in 66/685–6, the war-cry of his followers, we are told, was "*yā Manṣūr amit!*" —"O Manṣūr, kill."[23] The messianic character of Mukhtār's movement, and the strong Yemeni element among his supporters, are well known.[24] This slogan is an obvious appeal to Southern particularism, and to the messianic aspiration in which it found expression. In 81/700 another rebel, 'Abd al-Raḥmān b. Ash'ath, is said to have announced himself as the Qaḥṭānī, awaited by the Yemenites to restore their power; the poetess Bint Sahm called him al-Manṣūr 'Abd al-Raḥmān.[25] In 121/739, when the Shī'a appealed to Zayd b. 'Alī to rise in revolt, they said: 'We desire that you be the Manṣūr, and that this be the time in which the Umayyads perish.'[26] Most striking of all is the account of the beginnings, in Ramaḍān 129/June 747, of the final revolt, which culminated in the overthrow of the Umayyads and the establishment of the Abbasids. When the first followers of Abū Muslim in Khurāsān declared themselves, they did so by raising the black flags and by shouting '*yā Muḥammad, yā Manṣūr.*'[27]

The association of these two acts, together with the evidence of earlier revolts on the one hand, and of South Arabian tradition on the other, shows quite conclusively that the adoption of the title al-Manṣūr by the second Abbasid Caliph represented an appeal to messianic aspirations, and that this title was of the same character as those used by his two predecessors and his two successors. The specifically Southern Arabian connotation of this title raises further interesting questions—concerning the nature of Abbasid support, and the extent to which the Abbasid *daʿwa* and other religious opposition movements before it, appealed directly to southern resentments against the northern tribe.

The messianic implications of the title al-Manṣūr did not disappear with its adoption by the second Abbasid Caliph. An undated silver dirham of the late 2nd or early 3rd/early 9th century, struck by an unknown rebel, bears the inscription *Yā ḥamd ṣalla allāhu ʿalā Muḥammad ʿalayhi al-salām mimmā amara bihi al-Mahdī al-haqq amīr al-muʾminīn yā Manṣūr.*[28] The association of the titles Mahdī and Manṣūr with a claim to the Caliphate speaks for itself. At a later date, the title was still used by the Ismāʿīlīs. The *dāʿī* Ibn Ḥawshab, sent to the Yemen in ca. 268/881–2, adopted the title Manṣūr al-Yaman, no doubt to appeal to local sentiments,[29] and in 334/945 the third Fatimid Caliph in North Africa after al-Mahdī and al-Qāʾim succeeded to the Caliphate with the title al-Manṣūr. Thereafter the name seems to have lost its special significance and was adopted by many Muslim rulers.

The first five leaders of the Abbasid cause, one pretender and four Caliphs, all have titles of messianic import. Their claim to leadership, as the kin of the Prophet, *ahl al-bayt*, was couched in religious terms; their appeal was to deep-rooted anxieties and passions, to the burning belief, expressed in and encouraged by popular prophecies in the imminent coming of a rightful leader who would end tyranny and inaugurate a new age of justice and plenty. By conforming to the signs and portents of the approaching golden age, and adopting the titles of the divinely appointed ruler who, in God's good time, would lead mankind into it, they tried to persuade men that their advent was indeed the fulfillment of the prophecies, the final achievement of God's purpose on earth. In this way they sought to gain, first, support for their revolutionary attempt to seize power, and then, after the victory, consent to their legitimate retention of the power they had seized. Four times[30] the millennium was deferred to the next reign—to a new just ruler, with a new messianic title, until the process was no longer feasible or even necessary. The new imperial dynasty was firmly in control; the revolutionary leaders were safely dead; the charisma, in Max Weber's phrase, was routinized. The Abbasids, like other successful revolutionaries before and after them, chose the path of orthodoxy and empire. Some of their disappointed followers turned away, to fresh illusions and disillusionments; others found their place, as best they could, in the new imperial order. Of the revolutionary and messianic origins of the Abbasid movement, only the outward forms remained. The radical beliefs gave way to pious conformity; the black emblems of revolution became a dynastic livery; the messianic war-cries became part of the style and titles of imperial protocol.

Chapter Nine

“Daftar”

Register

"Daftar"
Register

Daftar, a stitched or bound booklet, or register, more especially an account or letter-book used in administrative offices. The word derives ultimately from the Greek διπθερα "hide", and hence prepared hide for writing. It was already used in ancient Greek in the sense of parchment or, more generally, writing materials. In the 5th century B.C. Herodotus[1] remarks that the Ionians, like certain barbarians of his own day, had formerly written on skins, and still applied the 'term *diphthera* to papyrus rolls; in the 4th Ctesias[2] claimed, somewhat unconvincingly, to have based his stories on the βασιλικαι διφθεραι—presumably the royal archives—of Persia. The word also occurs in pre-Islamic and even pre-Christian Jewish Aramaic texts.[3] Attempts to derive it from an Iranian root meaning to write (also found in *dabīr, dīwān*) are unconvincing; on the other hand, in view of the testimony of the Arab authors, it is probable that the word reached Arabic via Persian.

I. The Classical Period

In early Islamic times *daftar* seems to have been used to denote the codex form of book or booklet, as opposed to rolls and loose sheets. It was at first applied to quires and notebooks, especially those said to have been kept by some collectors of traditions as an aid to their memories; later, when sizable manuscript books come into existence, it was applied to them also.[4]

The creation of the first Islamic record office is usually ascribed to the Caliph ʻUmar, who instituted the muster-rolls and pay-rolls of the fighting-men. The initial form of these is not known, but before long they were probably kept on papyrus, which after the conquest of Egypt became the usual writing material in the administrative offices of the Caliphate. The papyri show that records of land, population, and taxes were kept in Egypt; surviving documents include quires as well as rolls and loose sheets, though the latter seem to have been the usual form, and no quire in Arabic appears until a comparatively late date.[5] In general, the Umayyad Caliphs seem to have followed Byzantine bureaucratic practices, and kept their records on papyrus. This did not lend itself to the codex form.

There was, however, also another bureaucratic tradition. The Sāsānids clearly could not have relied on supplies of imported Egyptian papyrus for their administration, and made use of a variety of prepared skins as writing materials.[6] According to Ḥasan al-Qummī, quoting Hamadānī on the authority of al-Madā'inī,[7] the Sāsānid Emperor Kobād kept a land-tax office at Ḥulwān; this is indirectly confirmed by Yaʻqūbī's story[8] of the procuring, in Muʻāwiya's time, of lists of Sāsānid domain lands from Ḥulwān.[9] It is possible that some of the army lists of the earlier period, at least in the ex-Persian provinces, were already in codex form. Balādhurī[10] has ʻUmar say to the Banū ʻAdī "if the *daftar* is closed *(yuṭbaq)* on you", and explains it as meaning "if you are registered last". Abū Muslim is said to have prepared a pay-roll called *daftar* instead of the usual *dīwān* of his followers in Khurāsān in 129/766–7.[11] These may, of course, be no more than a projection backwards, by later historians, of a term common in their own time, though it is significant that the first example comes from the East. According to the bureaucratic tradition, it was Khālid b. Barmak who, during the reign of al-Saffāḥ, introduced the codex or register into the central administration. Until that time, says Jahshiyārī,[12] the records of the *dīwāns* were kept on *Ṣuḥuf;* Khālid was the first to keep them in *daftars.* Maqrīzī[13] goes further and says that the *Ṣuḥuf mudraja*[14] which had hitherto been used were replaced by *dafātir min al-julūd*—parchment codices.

In the time of Hārūn al-Rashīd, Khālid's grandson, Ja'far b. Yaḥyā al-Barmakī, was responsible, it is said, for the introduction of paper. In this story there is some element of exaggeration. An incident told by Jahshiyārī[15] shows that under Manṣūr papyrus was still much used in government offices, and the supply from Egypt a matter of concern; it was still used under Hārūn al-Rashīd, and even as late as the time of Mu'taṣim, an abortive attempt was made to set up a papyrus factory, with Egyptian workmen, in Sāmarrā.[16] It is, however, broadly true that from the accession of the 'Abbāsids the register in codex form came to be the normal method of keeping records and accounts in government offices. Its use was confirmed and extended with the general adoption of paper from the 9th century onwards, and from this time the term *daftar* is in the main confined to administrative registers and record-books.

The system of *daftars* seems to have been first elaborated in Iran and Iraq. In Egypt papyrus remained in use until the 4th/10th century, but the eastern form of *daftar* seems to have been introduced even before the general adoption of paper. Surviving specimens of papyrus account-books in quire form[17] tally fairly closely with literary descriptions of the *daftar* in eastern sources.[18] From Egypt the *daftar* spread to the western Islamic world. In 373/985, al-Muqaddasī found it worthy of note that the people of Andalusia had their account-books as well as their Qur'āns on parchment.

Types of Daftar

With the development of elaborate bureaucratic organizations, the keeping of *daftars* became a task calling for special skills and knowledge, and *daftars* of many different types emerge. The first systematic account that we possess of the records and registers of a Muslim administrative office is that given by Muḥammad b. Aḥmad al-Khwārizmī in the late 4th/10th century. He enumerates the following:

1. *Qānūn al-Kharāj*—the basic survey in accordance with which the *Kharāj* is collected.
2. *Al-Awāraj*—Arabicized form of *Awāra*, transferred; shows the debts owed by individual persons, according to the *Qānūn*, and the instalments paid until they are settled.[19]
3. *Al-Rūznāmaj*—day-book; the daily record of payments and receipts.
4. *Al-Khatma*—the statement of income and expenditure presented monthly by the *Jahbadh*.

5. *Al-Khatma al-Jāmi'a*—the annual statement.
6. *Al-Ta'rīj*—an addition register, showing those categories *(abwāb)* which need to be seen globally, arranged for easy addition, with totals. Receipts for payments made are also registered here.
7. *Al-'Arīḍa*—a subtraction register, for those categories where the difference between two figures needs to be shown. It is arranged in three columns, with the result in the third. Such is the *'Arīḍa* showing the difference between the original and the revised figures, the latter being usually smaller, that is, presumably, the estimates and the amounts actually received.[20] These are itemized in the first and second columns, with the differences between them in the third column. Grand totals are shown at the foot of each of the three columns.
8. *Al-Barā'a*—a receipt given by the *Jahbadh* or *Khāzin* to taxpayers. (It is not clear whether Khwārizmī means a register of copies and receipts, or is merely naming the *barā'a* as a kind of document).
9. *Al-Muwāfaqa wa'l-jamā'a*—a comprehensive accounting *(ḥisāb jāmi')* presented by an *'āmil* on relinquishing his appointment. If it is approved by the authority to whom he presents it, it is called *muwāfaqa,* if they differ, it is called *muḥāsaba.*

Passing to the registers of the army office *(dīwān al-jaysh),* Khwārizmī lists:

10. *Al-Jarīda al-Sawdā'*—prepared annually for each command, showing the names of the soldiers, with their pedigree *(nasab),* ethnic origin *(jins),*

physical descriptions (*ḥilya*), rations, pay etc. This is the basic central register of this *dīwān*.

11. *Raj'a*—a requisition (*ḥisāb*) issued by the paymaster (*mu'ṭī*) for certain troops stationed in outlying areas, for one issue of pay (*tama'*) on reference to the *dīwān*.
12. *Al-Raj'a al-jāmi'a*—a global requisition issued by the head of the army office for each general issue *(ṭama')* of army pay, rations, etc.
13. *Al-Ṣakk*—an inventory[21] required for every *ṭama'* showing the names of the payees, with numbers and amounts, and bearing the signed authority to pay of the sultan. The *ṣakk* is also required for the hire of muleteers and camel-drivers.
14. *Al-Mu'āmara*—an inventory of orders issued during the period of the *ṭama'*, bearing at its end a signed authorization *(ijāza)* by the sultan. A similar *mu'āmara* is prepared by every *dīwān*.
15. *Al-Istiqrār*—an inventory of the supplies remaining in hand after issues and payments have been made.
16. *Al-Muwāṣafa*—a list (*'amal)* showing the circumstances and causes of any changes occurring (*i.e.* transfers, dismissals, deaths, promotions, etc.).
17. *Al-Jarīda al-musajjala*—the sealed register. The *sijill* (seal) is the letter given to an envoy or messenger, authorizing him, on arrival, to recover the expenses of his journey from any *'āmil.* The *sijill* is also the judicial verdict *(maḥḍar)* prepared by a *qāḍī*.
18. *Al-Fihrist*—a repertory of the inventories and registers in the *dīwān*.
19. *Al-Dastūr*—a copy of the *jamā'a* made from the draft.

Finally, Khwārizmī gives the names of three registers *(daftar)* used by the scribes of Iraq. They are (as given in the edition)

1. الانجيذج
2. الاوشنج
3. الدروزن

The third is explained as a register of the land measurement survey *(misāḥa)*.[22] It is probable that Khwārizmī's account refers to Samanid rather than 'Abbāsid offices in this first instance. It is, however, almost certainly applicable in great part to 'Abbāsid administration, and much of what he says is attested by passing references in the historians of Iraq and Persia.

Khwārizmī's registers fall into two main groups, the fiscal and the military, which may now be considered separately.

Fiscal Registers

The most important register of the tax-office is the *Qānūn,* the survey of land and taxable crops.[23] This served as the basis for the assessment and collection of the land-tax and was thus the main instrument and authority for the department's activities. The term *Qānūn,* already recognized by Khwārizmī as arabicized Greek *(yūnāniyya mu'arraba),* was employed chiefly in Iraq and the East, and was still in use in the 13th and 14th centuries, when it designated a kind of cadastral and fiscal survey.[24] In later times the term *Qānūn* in this sense seems to have fallen out of use, and was replaced by others. In Egypt the term *mukallafa* was used to designate the land survey registers, which were prepared by a *māsiḥ* and arranged by villages.[25] According to Maqrīzī,[26] a new survey was made in Egypt every thirty years.[27]

The *Rūznāmaj* or *Rūznāmče* is mentioned in an anecdote attributed to the time of Yaḥyā b. Khālid al-Barmakī. A Persian taunts an Arab with the dependence of Arabic on Persian for terms and nomenclature, "even in your cookery, your drinks, and your *dīwāns,*" and cites the word *Rūznāmaj,* as an example in the last-named group.[28] A passage in Miskawayh throws some light on how the *Rūznāmaj* was kept, in the treasury, in early 4th/10th century Baghdad. In 315/927, he tells us, the wazīr 'Alī b. 'Īsā "relied on Ibrāhīm b. Ayyūb[29] to report to him on financial matters, to instruct the Treasurer *(Ṣāḥib bayt al-māl)* concerning his daily disbursements, and to require of him the weekly presentation of the *Rūznāmajāt,* so that he might quickly know what had been paid out, what received, and what the deficit was *(mā ḥalla wa-mā qabaḍa wa-mā baqiya).* The previous practice in making up the account *(khatma)* had been to present a monthly statement to the *dīwān* in the middle of the following month."[30]

Two other passages in the same work indicate that the functionary in the treasury whose task it was to prepare the *khatma* was the *Jahbadh.*[31] Two documents of the time of al-Muqtadir, quoted in the *Ta'rīkh-i Qumm*, shows how the *Rūznāmaj* functioned in Qumm and Fārs. Here the writer *(Kātib)* of the *Rūznāmāj* is distinct from the *jahbadh,* and is a government official. His task is to register the sums received in taxes and issue receipts, called *Barā'a*, and to act as a kind of auditor on the operations of the *Jahbadh.*[32] In Ayyūbid Egypt Ibn Mammātī still includes the preparation of the *Rūznāmaj* and the *Khatma* among the duties of the *Jahbadh*.[33]

Many scattered references to the *daftars* kept in 'Abbāsid offices will be found in the writings of Miskawayh, Hilāl, and others especially interested in administrative affairs. Some idea of the scale and presentation of the accounts of the state may be gathered from a few individual balance sheets of imperial revenue and expenditure that have been preserved by the historians. The earliest, dating from the time of Hārūn al-Rashīd, is preserved by Jahshiyārī[34] and, in a variant version by Ibn Khaldūn.[35]

Military Registers

The muster-rolls of fighting-men date back to the beginnings of the Islamic state. These tribal rolls were, however, of quite a different character from the regular army lists described by Khwārizmī. It may be that Abū Muslim was the first to introduce the *daftar* of soldiers; certainly the practice became general under the 'Abbāsids. Besides Khwārizmī's notes, we have a fuller description of the army lists kept in the *dīwān al-jaysh* in Qudāma's treatise on the land-tax, and in a late anonymous treatise on tactics.[36] Similar lists were kept in the *dīwān al-jaysh* and *dīwān al-rawātib* (army office and pay office) of the Fāṭimids in Egypt.[37] The common term for the army lists was *jarīda*.

Diplomatic Registers

Khwārizmī's description is confined to financial and statistical registers—to accounts, inventories and the like in the tax and pay offices. Besides these there were also letter-books and other diplomatic registers, used in the chancery offices. A description of those kept in the Fāṭimid chancery (*dīwān al-rasā'il*) is given by the Egyptian scribe Ibn al-Ṣayrafī (463–542/1070–1147). In the 12th chapter of his *Qānūn Dīwān al-Rasā'il*,[38] he considers the registers (*daftar*) and memoranda (*tadhkira*)[39] which should be kept in this office, and the qualities of their keeper. This, he says is one of the most important tasks in the *dīwān*. The registrar must be reliable, long-suffering, painstaking, and work-loving, and should keep the following memoranda and registers.

1. Memoranda (*tadhākīr*) of important matters (*muhimmāt al-umūr*) which have been dealt with in correspondence, and to which it may be necessary to refer. These memoranda (*tadhākīr*) are much easier for reference than papers in bundles (*aḍābīr;* Massé translates 'dossier'). All letters received must therefore, after being answered, be passed to the registrar, who will consider them and record what is needed in his memoranda, together with any reply sent. He will assign a number of sheets (*awrāq*) in his memoranda to each transaction (*ṣafqa*), with an appropriate heading. He will then register incoming letters, noting their provenance, date of arrival and contents, together with a note of the reply sent or, if such be the case, of the fact that no reply was sent. He will continue this to the end of the year, when he will start a new *tadhkira*.
2. Memoranda of important orders (*awāmir*) in outgoing letters, in which are noted also the contents and dates of arrival of replies received to them.

This is to ensure that orders are not disregarded and left unanswered.

3. A register (*daftar*) showing the correct forms of *inscriptio* (*alqāb*), *salutatio* (*du'ā'*), etc. to be used for various officials and dignitaries, as well as foreign rulers and other correspondents abroad, in different types of letters and diplomas. For each office or post (*khidma*) there should be a separate sheet (*waraqa mufrada*) showing the name of its occupant, his *laqab*, and his *du'ā'*. Changes and transfers must be carefully noted.
4. A register of major events (*al-ḥawādith al-'aẓīma*).
5. A specification (*tibyān*) of ceremonial (*tashrīfāt*) and robes of honour (*khil'a*), to serve as a model when required. This should show grants made, with sartorial details, and prices.
6. A repertory (*fihrist*), by year, month, and day, of incoming letters, showing provenance, date of arrival with a summary or, if needed, a transcript of the text.
7. The same for outgoing letters.
8. A repertory of diplomas, brevets, investitures, safe-conducts, etc. This is to be prepared monthly, accumulated yearly, and restarted each new year.

Finally, Ibn al-Ṣayrafī refers to the need to record Arabic translations of letters received in foreign scripts (*khaṭṭ*) such as Armenian, Greek or Frankish.

According to Qalqashandī,[40] these Fāṭimid registers were in general maintained in the Cairo chancery until the end of the 8th/14th century. It is clear that this system of chancery registration and records originated in the eastern lands of the Caliphate, and continued there in one form or another, through the Middle Ages. Its later development can be seen in the Ottoman *Mühimme Defteri, Aḥkām, Tewjīhāt Defteri, Teshrifātjī Ḳalemi Defteri*, etc.

II. The Turkish and Mongol Period

In bureaucratic practice, as is in most other aspects of government and administration, the period of domination by the Steppe peoples, Turks and Mongols, brought noteworthy changes. Some of these may be due to Chinese influences, penetrating through the Uygurs, the Karakhitay, and above all through the Asian Empire of the Mongols. It seems likely that the system of registration owes something to East Asian examples,[41] but this whole question is still in need of further investigation.

Despite some evidence of reorganization under the Great Seljuks, the registrars and book-keepers of the Sultanate, as well as of Seljukid Anatolia and Ayyūbid Egypt, seem to have continued many of the practices of the preceding period. What development there is seems to be in technical matters, especially in the collection and presentation of statistical data. Some idea of bureaucratic practice in the Sultanate of Rūm can be obtained from Ibn Bībī, *Al-Awāmir al-'Alā'iyya*, facsimile ed. Ankara 1956.[42] Registers were kept at the Dīwān-i A'lā, and dealt with land and tax matters. As new territories were acquired or recovered, new surveys were conducted.[43] An addition by Yazijioghlu[44] tells that during the reign of 'Izz al-Dīn Kaykāwūs the office of *Ṣāḥib-i Dīwān* and the care of the finance registers (*emwāl defātiri*) were entrusted to Khwāja Badr al-Dīn Khurāsānī, "who was unequalled in the lands of Rūm in his knowledge of *khaṭṭ, balāgha, inshā', siyāqat,* and *ḥisāb*.'" At the same time Khwāja Fakhr al-Dīn 'Alī Tabrīzī was put in charge of *inshā'* and *maktūbāt*, and each of the 12 *daftars* in the *dīwān-i wizārat* entrusted to a competent master (*ustād*). On another occasion the office of *amīr-i 'āriḍ* was entrusted to Shams al-Dīn, also a specialist in *inshā'* and *siyāqat*,[45] Yazijioghlu adds the explanation that this office involved the control of the military registers (*čeri defteri*).[46] Another passage in the same work[47] speaks of 24 registrars, 12 in the *dīwān-i wizārat* dealing with land and taxes, and 12 in the *dīwān-i ᶜāriḍ* dealing with the lists of soldiers, pay and fiefs. A poem cited by Yazijioghlu,[48] repeats these figures, but awakens doubt of their authenticity by linking them with the recurring figure 12 in the Oghuz legend. The same poem claims complete coverage in the registration of lands.[49]

From the Il–Khānid period we have, for the first time, detailed treatises on public accounting. Two important works, the *Sa'ādat-nāma* of Falak 'Alā-i Tabrīzī (compiled 707/1307) and the *Risāla-i Falakiyya* of 'Abd Allah b. Muḥammad b. Kiyā al-Māzandarānī (ca.767/1363) were discovered and analysed by Zeki Velidi [Togan].[50] A Tīmūrid manual, written in Herāt ca. 845/1441, was discovered by Adnan Erzi[51] and a complete budget (*Jāmi' al-Ḥisāb*) of 738/1337–8 found by Z. V. Togan. The first two were studied in great detail by W. Hinz (in *Das Rechnungswesen*), to whom we also owe a critical edition of the second of them.[52]

These works reveal a system of book-keeping based on seven main registers, as follows:

1. *Rūznāma*—'Daybook,' Arabicized from *Rūznāmaj*, also called *Daftar-i Ta'līq*.
2. *Daftar-i Awāraja*—cash-book, showing the balance of moneys in hand.
3. *Daftar-i Tawjīhāt*—register of disbursements.
4. *Daftar-i Taḥwīlāt*—an off-shoot of the preceding, dealing with disbursements for stocks and running expenses in state establishments and enterprises.
5. *Daftar-i Mufradāt*—budget register showing the income and expenditure by cities, districts, and provinces.
6. *Jāmi' al-Ḥisāb*—the master-ledger, from which the annual financial reports were prepared.

Qānūn—the survey and assessment book, or Domesday Book of the Empire.[53]

III. The Post-Mongol States

As in so many other respects, the Muslim states of the post-Mongol period seem to have followed, to a very large extent, the bureaucratic practices of the Il-Khāns, some of which can be recognized as far afield as Mamluk Cairo, Ottoman Istanbul and Mughal Delhi. Of these states only one, the Ottoman Empire, has left a collection of registers that has survived to the present day, though individual *daftars* have come to light in other parts. The Ottoman *daftars* have been discussed elsewhere, and need not, therefore, be described here.

Numbers of Ottoman registers have also come to light in the ex-Ottoman territories in Europe, Asia and Africa.[54]

Bibliography: For a general discussion see the unfortunately incomplete article of M. Cevdet, published in Osman Ergin's *Muallim M. Cevdet'in Hayatı, Eserleri ve Kütüphanesi*, Istanbul 1937, appendix, 69–96; on finance registers C. Leyerer, "Studien zum Rechnungswesen der arabischen Steuerämter," *ArO*, xii, 1941, 85–112; idem, "Die Verrechnung und Verwaltung von Steuern im islamischen Ägypten," *ZDMG*, N.F. 28, 1953, 40–69; W. Hinz, "Das Rechnungswesen orientalischer Reichsfinanzämter im Mittelalter," *Isl.*, xxix, 1950, 1–29, 113–141; on military registers W. Hoenerbach, "Zur Heeresverwaltung der Abbasiden," *ibid.*, 257–290. On Ottoman finance registers, L. Fekete, *Die Siyaqat-Schrift in der türkischen Finanzverwaltung*, i, Budapest 1955, 67–110; on the *Qāḍī's* registers Halit Ongan, *Ankara'nin I Numaralı Şer'iye Sicili*, Ankara 1958, and J. Kabrda, "Les anciens registres turcs des Cadis de Sofia et de Vidin," *ArO*, xix, 1951, 329–392; on Safavid Persia V. Minorsky, *Tadhkirat al-Mulūk*, London, 1943; on Central Asia, M. Yuldashev, "*The State Archives of XIX century feudal Khiva*," in *Papers presented by the Soviet delegation at the XXIII International Congress of Orientalists: Iranian, Armenian and Central Asian Studies*, Moscow 1954, 221–30. Some *daftars* have been published in full. The earliest Ottoman survey register was edited by H. Inalcik, *Hicri* 835 *Tarihli Sûret-i Defter-i Sancak-i Arvanid*, Ankara 1954; an Ottoman survey register of Georgia was edited by S. Jikia, *Gurjistanis vilaiethis didi davthari. Defteri mufassali vilâyeti Gürcüstan.* Great register of the vilayet of Gurjistan. Vol. 1, Turkish text. Vol. 2, Georgian translation. Izdatel'stvo Akademii Nauk Gruzinskoy SSR: Tiflis, 1941–1947.

Chapter Ten

"Dīwān-i Humāyūn"
The Ottoman Imperial Council

"Dīwān-i Humāyūn"
The Ottoman Imperial Council

Dīwān-i humāyūn, the name given to the Ottoman imperial council, until the mid 11th/17th century the central organ of the government of the Empire. Evidence on the *dīwān* under the early Sultans is scanty. According to 'Āshiḳpashazāde,[1] the practice of wearing a twisted turban (*burma dülbend*) when attending the *dīwān* was introduced during the reign of Orkhān. Probably a kind of public audience is meant. The Egyptian physician Shams al-Dīn b. Ṣaghīr, sent by Barqūq to treat Bāyazīd II, describes how the Ottoman ruler used to hold public audience in the morning and dispense justice to the people.[2]

'Āshiḳpashazāde[3] speaks of the pashas holding a *dīwān* when Meḥemmed I was dying, and of a daily *dīwān* at the Porte (*ḳapu),* and again[4] of a similar *dīwān* of the pashas on the death of Murād II. From these, and parallel narratives in Neshrī and other early chroniclers, it may be inferred that by the early 9th/15th century it had become a regular practice for the Sultan to preside over a council of the pashas, and that during the interregnum between the death of a Sultan and the arrival of his successor the *dīwān* could, exceptionally, be held by the pashas on their own. Meḥemmed II seems to have been the first Sultan to give up the practice of presiding over the meetings of the *dīwān,* relinquishing this function to the Grand Vizier. According to an anecdote recorded by later historians the reason for this was that a peasant with a grievance came to the *dīwān* one day and said to the assembled dignitaries: "Which of you is the Sultan? I have a complaint." The Sultan was offended, and the Grand Vizier Gedik Aḥmed Pasha suggested to him that he might avoid such embarrassments by not appearing at the *dīwān*. Instead, he could observe the proceedings from behind a grille or screen[5]. Whatever the truth of the anecdote, the withdrawal of the Sultan is confirmed by the *Ḳānūn* of Meḥemmed II, which states clearly that the Sultan sits behind a screen (*janāb-i sherīfim peṣ-i perdede oturup*).[6] This practice continued until the time of Suleymān Ḳānūnī, who ceased to attend the meetings of the *dīwān* even in this form.[7]

Constitution and procedure. The *Ḳānūn* of Meḥemmed II, which purports to set forth the practice of the Sultan's father and grandfather, lays down the constitution of the *dīwān-i humāyūn* in some detail. The *dīwān* met every day; those attending were, in order of precedence, the Grand Vizier, the other viziers, the ḳāḍī'askers, the defterdārs, and the nishānji. If the nishānji had the rank of vizier or beylerbey, he sat above the defterdars; if that of sanjaḳ-beyi, below the defterdārs. When they came, they were received with obeissance by the Chief Pursuivant (*Ča'ush-bashı*) and by the Intendant of the Doorkeepers (*Ḳapıjılar Kâhyası*). Four times a week a meeting was held in the audience chamber (*arḍ odasi*), attended by the viziers, ḳāḍī'askers, and defterdārs, at which the Sultan was present behind a grille.[8] In former times, it had been the practice of the Sultans to dine with the viziers, but Meḥemmed had abolished this.[9]

In the course of the 10th/16th century the membership of the *dīwān* was somewhat extended. A document of 942/1536, quoted by Ferīdūn[10] authorizes the Beylerbey of Rumeli to attend the *dīwān* but excludes the Beylerbey of Anatolia. Later, in recognition of the growing importance of naval affairs, the Ḳapudān Pasha was added. The Agha of the Janissaries, however, was only a member if he held the rank of vizier. Besides the full members of the *dīwān,* a number of other dignitaries were in attendance, though they had no seats in the council-chamber and did not participate in the deliberations. Among these were the Chief Secretary (*re'īs al-kuttāb*), head of the chancellery; the Chief Pursuivant; the Intendant of the Doorkeepers, who maintained liaison between the Grand Vizier and the Sultan; the financial secretaries (*muḥāsaba*); the *dīwān* interpreters (*terjumān*); the police chiefs (*shurṭa*), and a number of other palace and administrative officers who might be called upon to carry out the decisions of the *dīwān,* with their assistants, clerks, and messengers.

During the 10th/16th century, the *dīwān* met regularly four times a week, on Saturday, Sunday, Monday and Tuesday. Its proceedings began at daybreak, and dealt with the whole range of government business. The morning was normally devoted to public sessions, and especially the hearing of petitions and complaints, which were adjudicated by the relevant member of the *dīwān,* or by the Grand Vizier himself. About noon, the mass of petitioners and other outside visitors withdrew, and lunch was served to the members of the *dīwān*, who then proceeded to discuss what business remained. Withers (after Bon) makes it clear that the council was purely consultative, the final responsibility resting with the Grand Vizier: "Dinner being ended, the chief Vizier spendeth some small time about general affairs, and taking counsel together (if he pleaseth and thinks it fit) with the other Bashaws; at last he determineth and resolveth of all within himself, and prepareth to go in unto the King (it being the ordinary custom so to do, in two of the four Divan days, *viz.* upon Sunday, and upon Tuesday) to render an account briefly unto his Majesty of all such businesses as he hath dispatched."[11] Besides the regular *dīwān* meetings, certain special *dīwāns* were held. These were 1) the *'ulūfe dīwāni or ghalebe dīwāni,* held quarterly for the distribution of pay and supplies to the Janissaries and other 'slaves of the gate', and also for the reception of foreign ambassadors, 2) the *ayak dīwānı*—foot *dīwān*—an extraordinary or emergency meeting presided over by the Sultan or army-commander. It was so-called because all present remained standing.[12]

Place of meeting. The *dīwān* building, usually known as *dīwānkhāne,* stands in the second court of the Topḳapu palace, between the Middle gate *(Ortaḳapu)* and the Gate of Felicity *(Bāb al-se'āde).* The present structure was erected during the reign of Suleymān Ḳānūnī, by order of the Grand Vizier Ibrāhīm Pasha, and repaired in 1792 and 1819. In earlier times the *dīwān* met in another building, later referred to as the 'old *dīwānkhāne'*. The council chamber was known as *ḳubbe-alti,* 'under the dome', and those viziers who had the right to attend the *dīwān* were called 'the dome viziers'. Overlooking the council-chamber was a screened enclosure known as the *ḳaṣr-i 'ādil* or *ḳafes,* from which the Sultan could observe the proceedings. This was directly connected with the *ḥarem* quarters. Adjoining the *dīwānkhāne* were the offices and quarters of the various viziers, and the office of the Grand Vizier, known as *Divit (=dawāt) odasi.*[13]

Administration. The main branches of the central administration, functioning under the *dīwān-i humāyūn,* were as follows:

(1) *Dīwān Ḳalemi,* also called *Beylik* or *Beylikji ḳalemi,* the central chancery office, headed by the *Beylikji,* the senior chancery officer under the *re'īs al-kuttāb.* This office was responsible for drafting, issuing, and filing copies of all edicts, regulations *(Ḳānūn),* decrees and orders other than those concerned with finance. Treaties, capitulations, privileges and exequaturs issued to foreign powers were also, for a time, the concern of this department.

Besides the chancery, there were two departments dealing with questions of personnel, *viz:*

(2) the *Tahwīl Ḳalemi,* also called *nishān* or *kese ḳalemi,* which issued orders and kept records on appointments to the rank of vizier, beylerbey, sanjaḳ-beyi, and *mawlā—i.e., ḳāḍī* of a *wilāyet,* as well as appointments and transfers to *timars* and *zi'āmets.*

(3) the *Ru'ūs ḳalemi,* which was concerned with appointments to all ranks and posts other than those covered by the *Taḥwīl ḳalemi,* the emoluments of which came from treasury or *waḳf* funds. These included religious as well as civil and military posts.

Apart from these three main offices, there were two other branches, headed by the *Teshrīfātji* and the

Waḳ'anuwīs, dealing respectively with ceremonial and with historical records. A later addition was the office of the *Āmedī* or *Āmedji,* who headed the personal staff of the *Re'īs al-kuttāb*. This was concerned with the conduct of relations with foreign states, and with the maintenance of liaison between government departments and the palace.

Some of the staff employed in these offices received salaries; others, of lower status, were paid with *tīmārs* and *zi'āmets*. The latter could be promoted to salaried appointments. The more important established officials had the rank of *khwājegān*. Their subordinates were called *khalīfe*.

Decline of the *dīwān-i humāyūn*. The growing importance of the Grand Vizierate as against the palace led to the practice of the *ikindi dīwānī,* a meeting held in the Grand Vizier's residence after the afternoon prayer (*ikindi*), to deal with unfinished business left over from the *dīwān-i humāyūn*. This body came to meet five times a week, and gradually took over a large part of the real work of the *dīwān-i humāyūn*. The transfer of the effective control and conduct of affairs from the palace to the Grand Vizierate was formalized in 1054/1654, when Sultan Meḥemmed IV presented the Grand Vizier Derwīsh Meḥmed Pasha with a building that served both as residence and as office. To this new institution most of the administrative departments formerly under the *dīwān-i humāyūn* were, in time, transferred. By the 18th century the *dīwān-i humāyūn* had dwindled into insignificance. A new form of *dīwān* appeared under the reforming sultans Selīm III and Mahmūd II, who established special councils to plan and apply the reforming edicts (*tanẓīmāt*). These in time evolved into a system of cabinet government.

Bibliography: an early statement, from an Ottoman official source, on the constitution and functioning of the *dīwān-i humāyūn* will be found in the Ḳānūn of Meḥemmed II, dealing with the officers and organization of the government *(Ḳānūnnāme-i āl-i 'Othmān,* ed. Meḥmed 'Ārif, *TOEM* Supplement 1330 A.H. 13ff.; 23 ff. The existing copy contains revisions dating from the reign of Bāyazīd II). This description may be supplemented from information in the Ottoman chronicles (notably the *Hasht Bihisht* of Idrīs Bidlīsī, reign of Meḥemmed II), and the foreign sources *(e.g.*, G.M. Angiolello [Donado da Lezze] *Historia turchesca,* ed. I. Ursu, Bucarest 1909, 130 ff.). The subsequent development of the institution may be traced in later *ḳānūns* (*e.g.*, that of 1087/1676, published in *MTM,* i/3, (1331 A.H.), 506 ff.) and later foreign descriptions (*e.g.,* the very full account written by the Venetian Bailo Ottaviano Bon in 1608, *Il Serraglio del gran Signore,* in N. Barozzi and G. Berchet, edd., *Relazioni degli stati europei lette al Senato* ..., 5 ser., i, Venice 1866 (English adaptation by Robert Withers, "A Description of the Grand Signiors Serraglio" in *Purchas His Pilgrimes,* London 1625, repr. Glasgow 1905, 322ff.; also in John Greaves, *Miscellaneous Tracts* ..., ii, London 1650 and later reprints), P. Rycaut, *History of the present state of the Ottoman Empire,* London 1675, Bk i, ch. Xi, 77 ff. From about the middle of the 10th/16th century, the development and functioning of the *dīwān-i humāyūn* and the various administrative departments and services which it controlled can be followed in great detail in the records preserved in the Ottoman archives. A classification and description will be found in Midhat Sertoğlu, *Muhteva bakımından başvekâlet arşivi,* Ankara 1955, 13–14. The fullest general description of the *dīwān-i humāyūn* and its administration is that of I. H. Uzunçarşılı, *Osmanlı devletinin merkez ve bahriye teşkilâti,* Ankara 1948, 1–110. Briefer accounts will be found in Jewdet[2], I, 43 6 (summarizing Wāṣif); D'Ohsson, *Tableau général de l'empire othoman,* vii, Paris 1824, 211–32; Hammer-Purgstall, *Staatsverfassung, 412–36;* idem, *Geschichte de osmanischen Reiches,* index; A. H. Lybyer, *The government of the Ottoman Empire in the time of Suleiman the Magnificent,* Cambridge Mass. 1913, 187–93; Zinkeisen,*Geschichte des osmanischen Reiches,* iii, Gotha 1855, 117–25; Gibb-Bowen, i/I, 115 ff. and index; Pakalın, i, 462–6, including a passage from the unpublished *Ḳawānīn-i teshrīfāt* of Nā'ilī 'Abd Allāh Pasha (d.1171/1757); Sertoğlu, *Resimli Osmanlı tarihi ansiklopedisi,* Istanbul 1958, 78–81. On the early Ottoman and Seljukid background, see I. H. Uzunçarşılı, *Osmanlı devleti Teşkilâtına medhal,* Istanbul 1941, 42–4, 95–8; V. A. Gordlevsky, *Izbrannie Sočineniya, i,* Moscow 1960, 166–77; Mustafa Akdağ, *Türkiye'nin iktisadi ve ictimaī tarihi,* i, 1243–1453, Ankara 1959, 217–23, 323–33.

Chapter Eleven

"Jumhūriyya"
Republic

"Jumhūriyya"
Republic

Jumhūriyya, in Turkish *cümhuriyet*, republic, also republicanism, a term coined in Turkey in the late 18th century from the Arabic *jumhūr*, meaning the crowd, mass, or generality of the people, and first used in connexion with the first French Republic. In classical Arabic, as for example in Arabic versions and discussions of Greek political writings, the usual equivalent of the Greek *politeia* or Latin *res publica*, *i.e.*, polity or commonweal, was *madīna*; thus the 'democratic polity' of Plato's classification is called, by Fārābī, and others, *madīna jamā'iyya*.[1] According to the law as stated by the Sunnī jurists, the Islamic polity itself was to be headed by a non-hereditary, elective sovereign, subject to and not above the law. This principle has led some 19th and 20th century writers to describe the Islamic doctrine of the Caliphate as republican.[2] Others, perhaps under the influence of recent developments in the use of the term, have gone further, and described the government of the patriarchal caliphs as a republic. In the more technical sense of a state in which the head holds his place by the choice of a defined electorate exercised through prescribed legal processes, the term republic seems to have no precise equivalent in classical Islamic usage. Such states existed and were encountered in Europe, in Ragusa, Venice and other Italian city republics. Arabic seems to have used no special term for them; thus Qalqashandī, speaking of the government of Genoa, calls them a *jamāʿa mutafāwitū 'l-marātib*; for Venice he speaks only of the Doge.[3] Turkish used *jumhūr*. Perhaps this was the word chosen by the dragomans of the Porte as equivalent, for official usage, to the Latin *res publica*. Thus, *Venedik jumhūru* was the formal translation of 'Republic of Venice.' Even so, the word *jumhūr* was comparatively rare in the sense of republic; more commonly the Turks, in their letters to Venice and their discussions of Venetian affairs, preferred to speak of the Doge (Venedik Dozhu) or signoria (Venedik Beyleri) rather than of the Republic.

The word *jumhūr* took on new life after the French Revolution, when it was used in Turkish to denote the French Republic as well as other republics—some of them on the borders of Turkey—that were formed on the French model. In Egypt, some of the translators attached to General Bonaparte's expedition, groping for an Arabic equivalent for republic chose *mashyakha*.[4] This term is recorded by some subsequent Arabic lexicographers, and was used of the French Republic by Ḥaydar al-Shihābī (d. 1835)[5] and others. It was not, however, confirmed by subsequent usage. The documents of the French occupation of Egypt, as cited by Ḥaydar himself[6] and by Niḳūlā al-Turk[7] and al-Jabartī[8] prefer the Ottoman term *jumhūr*, and speak of *al-jumhūr al-Faransāwī*.

The modern word *jumhūriyya*—which is simply *jumhūr* with an abstract ending—was coined; like many other Islamic neologisms, in Turkey, the first Islamic state to encounter the ideas, institutions and problems of the modern world, and to seek and find new terms to denote them. It was at first used as an abstract noun denoting a principle or form of government, and meaning republicanism rather than republic, the usual term for which was still *jumhūr*.[9] From Turkey the term spread to the Arabs, Persians, Indians, and other peoples, and was used in the new political literature inspired by western liberal and constitutional ideas. In the 19th century republic and democracy were still regarded as broadly synonymous terms, and the same words were often used for both. It is instructive to trace the renderings of the terms democracy and republic in the 19th century dictionaries from English or French into Arabic, Turkish etc. Bocthor (1828) translates the two terms by *Qiyām al-jumhūr bi'l-ḥukm* and *jumhūr* or *mashyakha*; Handjeri (1840) by *ḥukūmat al-jumhūr al-nās* [*sic*] and *jumhūr*, Redhouse (1860) translates democracy as *jümhūr*, or *jümhūriyyet uṣūlu,* republic as *jümhūr*, and republicanism as *jumhūriyyet*. Zenker (1866) and Sami Frasheri (1883) already identify *jümhūriyyet* with republic. In Urdu the same word, with a minor variation, has served both for democracry (*jumhūriyyat*) and republic (*jumhūriyya*).

Republican ideas are rarely expressed in the writings of the 19th century Muslim liberals, even the most radical of whom seem to have thought in terms of a constitutional monarchy rather than a republic. Even where the terms *jumhūrī* and *jumhūriyya* do occur, they often connote popular and representative rather than republican government.[10] During the 20th century, however, republicanism developed rapidly. The first republics to be established were in the Muslim territories of the Russian Empire, when the temporary relaxation of pressure from the center after the revolutions of 1917 allowed an interval of local experimentation. In May 1918, after the dissolution of the short-lived Transcaucasian Federation, the Azerbaijani members of the former Transcaucasian parliament, together with the Muslim National Council, declared Azerbaijan an independent republic—the first Muslim republic in modern times. In April 1920 it was conquered by the Red Army, and a Soviet Republic formed. The same pattern was followed by the Bashkirs and other Turkic peoples of the Russian Empire, who set up their own national republics, all of which were in due course taken over and reconstituted by the communists, and incorporated, in one form or another, in the U.S.S.R.

The first Muslim republic to be established outside the Russian Empire seems to have been the Tripolitanian Republic, proclaimed in November 1918 by Sulaymān Pasha al-Bārūnī,[11] and later incorporated in the Italian colony of Libya. The first independent republic to remain both independent and a republic was that of Turkey, proclaimed on 29 October 1923.[12] In Syria-Lebanon republican ideas were current in some circles at an earlier date, and the forms of government set up by the French as mandatory power were generally republican in tendency. The republics were not, however, formally constituted until some years later; Greater Lebanon was proclaimed a republic on 23 May 1926, Syria on 22 May 1930.

The ending of West European colonial rule in Islamic lands after the second World War brought several new republics into being. The republic of Indonesia was proclaimed in August 1945; Pakistan, independent since 1947, introduced a new theme by declaring an 'Islamic Republic' in November 1953. In Africa, the Sudan became a republic on attaining independence in January 1956; Tunisia, already independent, abolished the monarchy and proclaimed a republic in May 1959. Among the older Arab states in the Middle East two new republics were established after the revolutionary overthrow of the existing monarchical régimes—in Egypt in June 1953, in Iraq in July 1958. A union of Egypt and Syria, called the United Arab Republic (*al-jumhūriyya al-'Arabiyya al-Muttaḥida*) was formed in February 1958 and dissolved in September 1961. The name United Arab Republic was for a while retained by Egypt. An anti-monarchist revolution began in the Yemen in September 1962. At the present time the majority of Muslim states are called republics, though the common designation covers a wide variety of political realities.

Chapter Twelve

On Modern Arabic Political Terms

On Modern Arabic Political Terms

During the past hundred years the Arabs, like many other peoples in Asia and Africa, have had to find new words for a series of political concepts and institutions alien to their own traditions and imposed or imported from outside. Drawn from European history and expressed in terms of European thought, the new political language was strange and difficult and remained so even when the structures themselves began to change. Arab history offered no precedents for the new facts and ideas; the wealth of the Arabic language seemed to lack words to denote or even adequately to describe them.

In devising its vocabulary of modern politics, Arabic has resorted to four main methods—borrowing, neologism, semantic rejuvenation, and loan-translation.

Of these, borrowing is the least important. In contrast to other languages such as Turkish and even colloquial Arabic, modern literary Arabic has accepted very few loanwords, and even these, while remaining lexically foreign, have usually been grammatically assimilated. Political loanwords came in the main with identifiably foreign referents. These may be institutions, like *barlamān*, parliament, presumably via French; functions, like *qunṣul,* consul (with *qunṣuliyya,* consulate); political movements or ideologies, like *balshafī,* Bolshevik, and *fāsh*[*ist*]*ī,* fascist. The former is now of rare occurrence; the latter is very extensively used, usually in a standardized collocation with *nāzī,* as a non-specific term of abuse for political and national opponents. Two loanwords of more general application are *diktātūrī* (also *dīktātūrī*), dictatorial, and *dīmūqrāṭī,* democratic, each with its corresponding abstract noun ending in *iyya. Diktātūrī,* a pejorative term for authoritarian government, is of limited usefulness in the Arab countries at the present time. *Dīmūqrāṭī* on the other hand is widely used with a very variable range of meaning, including elements derived from Eastern and Western Europe and from North and South America, as well as from indigenous tradition and experience.[1]

At first sight it may seem surprising that Arabic should have borrowed the word *dīmūqrāṭī.* The notion was not altogether new and could have been known to scholars through the Arabic versions and adaptations of Greek political writings, in which "democratic polity" is rendered *madīna jamā'iyya.* This literature was however little read in the nineteenth and early twentieth centuries, and those who did read it may be excused for failing to perceive the connection between the systems described by ancient and medieval philosophers and the ideas and practices which were called democratic in their own day.

The same observations can be made of such neologisms as *jumhūriyya,* republic. In classical Arabic, the usual equivalent of the Greek *politeia* or Latin *res publica* was *madīna,* a word of Aramaic provenance which originally meant a jurisdiction, then a country or district, and finally a city. This word was obviously too vague for precise political description. When, in late medieval times, the Arabic-speaking countries encountered functioning republics in Venice and elsewhere, they seem to have felt no need to devise any special term for them. It was not until the French Revolution that the Muslims, recognizing the emergence of a new political phenomenon, coined a new word to denote it.

This term, like many of the Arabic neologisms of the nineteenth century, was an Ottoman rather than an Arab creation. The Turks were the first Muslim ruling group to encounter the facts and read the literature of modern politics and therefore to feel the need for a new vocabulary for both discussion and administration. Turkish was the dominant language in the Ottoman Empire, in Central Asia and for a while even in Egypt and part of North Africa. When it gave way, it was usually to European languages—French, Russian, English, or Italian. Modern Arabic was thus a comparative latecomer and was able to make use of an important new vocabulary coined by Ottoman scholars, officials, and journalists. For educated Turks, Arabic was a classical language, on which they drew in the same way as West Europeans drew on Latin and Greek. Lexically, metaphysics and telephone are both Greek loanwords in English—but the historical and cultural difference between the two cases is obvious. Both have their equivalents among the Arabic words in Ottoman Turkish. Many, like metaphysics in English, are words borrowed from an earlier culture along with the ideas and objects which they denote. Others, like telephone, are new coinages for new referents. When such words are adopted back into their languages of etymological origin, they are lexical natives but semantic intruders. Such are *têlephônon* and *têlegraphima* in modern Greek; such too are a wide range of new terms in modern Arabic.

These repossessed neologisms comprise an important part of the modern Arabic political vocabulary. *Jumhūriyya,* at first republicanism and then simply republic, is an Ottoman coinage of the late eighteenth century. An Arabic term for republic produced at the time of the French occupation of Egypt, *mashyakha,* was not accepted into common usage and soon disappeared in this sense. Today *jumhūriyya* is the universally recognized word for republic in all the Arab lands.[2]

Two other Ottoman neologisms of great popularity at the present time are *qawmiyya,* nationalism, and *ishtirākiyya,* socialism. Both date from the nineteenth century and appear to be products of Turkish journalism. *Kavım* (from Arabic *Qawm*) is used in Turkish in the sense of tribe or people, often with a somewhat derogatory implication, rather like the French *peuplade. Kavmiyet* was at first used in a pejorative sense to mean tribalism, and thence factional, particularistic, or disruptive nationalism. Thus in 1870 Ali Suavi uses it when arguing against nationalism. For Muslims, he says, only religious identity is important. Religion unites them; nationalism would divide them.[3] The same line of argument is pursued by other anti-nationalist Turkish writers, of both pan-Islamic and Ottomanist opinions, and in 1913 Mehmet Akif gave it vigorous poetic expression.[4] In the same year Ahmed Naim published a book denouncing nationalism *(kavmiyet)* as "a foreign innovation as deadly to the body of Islam as cancer is to man."[5] Even the theoretician of Turkish nationalism, Ziya Gökalp, used *kavım* and *kavmiyet* to denote identity and solidarity based on ethnic affinity and thus at a more primitive level than nationality based on religion *(ümmet)* or culture *(millet)*.[6]

In Turkish *kavmiyet* remained on the whole derogatory and gradually fell into disuse. In Arabic, however, the word entered on a new phase of development. It appears in the proclamation published by the Sharīf Ḥusayn of the Hijāz in 1916[7] and thereafter becomes standard Arabic usage. More recently, it has been specialized to denote pan-Arab nationalism as against the national or rather patriotic loyalties of the individual Arab countries.

Socialism in nineteenth-century Turkish was *ishtirāk-i emvāl*, literally "sharing of property," whence *ishtirakji,* a socialist, and *ishtiraki,* socialistic. In Turkish the term fell into disuse and was replaced by *Sosyalist.* Adopted in Arabic, it soon gained universal acceptance.

Other Ottoman Arabic neologisms include learned expressions, such as *iqtiṣādī,* economic, and a wide range of public administrative terms, such as *khārijiyya,* foreign affairs; *dākhiliyya,* home affairs; and *baladiyya,* municipality.

Apart from Ottoman usage, Arabic neologisms come from two main sources—Egypt and the Arabic-speaking Christians, especially the Maronites in Lebanon and elsewhere. They include such terms as *'ilmāni,* from *'alamānī* (earlier *'ālamānī*), secular (from *'ālam,* world, whence worldly); *shuyū'ī,* communist (from *shuyū'* or *shiyā'*, a legal term for community of property ownership); *duwalī,* international (derived, contrary to accepted grammatical usage, from the broken plural of *dawla,* state); *iqṭā'ī,* feudal (from *iqṭā'*, a grant of revenue to an officer or functionary in medieval Islamic states); *raj'ī,* reactionary (from *raja'a,* to return or turn back); *di'āya,* propaganda (from *da'ā,* to call or summon, a term technically applied to the preaching of certain sectarian missionaries in medieval Islam). Most of these words date from the late nineteenth or early twentieth century.

Another method of devising new terms is by a process of semantic rejuvenation or resemanticization. This occurs where an old word, which may or may not be obsolete, is given, more or less arbitrarily, a new meaning different from those which it previously expressed. Two examples, both from the nineteenth century, are *ḥukūma,* government, and *dustūr,* constitution.[8] In classical Arabic *ḥukūma* was a noun of action, meaning the act, later also the function, of adjudicating, of dispensing justice, whether by an arbitrator, a judge, or a ruler. After some semantic development, it was adopted in early nineteenth-century Turkish to express the European notion of government, that is, the group of men exercising the authority of the state, as distinct from the abstraction of the state on the one hand and the person of the sovereign on the other. In this sense it passed into Arabic and became common usage in the late nineteenth century.

Dustūr comes from a Persian word, originally meaning a person exercising authority, more particularly a member of the Zoroastrian priesthood. In classical Arabic usage, it had several meanings but commonly meant a rule or set of rules, especially in the craft-guilds. Its modern use in the sense of constitution is no doubt a development of this last meaning.

Other more recent refurbishments of old words include *shu'ūbiyya,* local (in other words, not pan-Arab) particularism (originally an anti-Arab faction in medieval times); *fidā'ī,* guerrilla or commando (literally one who offers his life as ransom, especially used of the terrorists sent out by the medieval Islamic sect known as the Assassins); *thawra,* revolution, originally rising, from the verb *thāra,* to rise, at first in the physical sense, for example—to quote examples given by classical lexicographers—a camel rising to its feet, a swarm of locusts rising into the air, and thence by extension an insurrection.

It is tempting to include such words as *umma,* nation, and *sha'b,* people, in this category, since their content at the present time differs radically from classical and even early modern Arabic usage. They might however more properly be placed in the fourth category, of loan-translation or calque.

This is, at the present time, by far the most usual method of procuring new terms and accounts for the greater part of the modern Arabic technical vocabulary, of politics as of other fields of activity and themes of discussion. Briefly, loan-translation means that an Arabic word is given a change of meaning or an extension of range of reference, borrowed from the historical development of the equivalent word in another language. Loan-translations occur even in classical Arabic—for example, in the terms *umm al-qurā,* "mother of towns," from the Greek *mêtropolis,* and *tadbīr al-manzil,* "management of the house," economy, from the Greek *oikonomía.* In modern times they have hitherto usually been drawn from English or French. One or two simple examples may suffice to explain the process. *Kahrabā'* in classical Arabic means amber, in modern Arabic electricity. This reproduces the development of the western word, which comes from the ancient Greek *êlektros*—amber. *Adhā'a* in classical Arabic means to spread or disseminate news or information, that is, to broadcast in the pre-technical English sense of the word. In modern Arabic it has imitated the development of the English word and acquired the meaning of public radio transmission.

Loan-translation of political terms takes several forms. The earliest examples are common Islamic political terms, used with a change of meaning of which the users were probably unaware. Thus, according to the dictionaries, *malik* means king and *wazīr* means minister—but the use of these words for nineteenth-century European or European-style monarchs and the members of their governments represented a substantial modification of the hitherto accepted connotation of these terms among Arabic-speakers. The same is true of such other terms as *umma,* religio-political community, nation; *dawla*, dynasty, government, state; *ra'īs,* head, chief, president, *ḥizb,* faction, group, party; *istiqlāl,* unrestricted rule, independence; *za'īm*, surety, pretender, leader.

The last of these is particularly interesting. In early classical Arabic *za'īm* had the meanings of leader, spokesman, or surety. In medieval practice it was used chiefly of rulers or claimants whose claims the user did not recognize. It was thus applied by Sunnī authors to the chiefs of the Ismā'īlī sectaries in Persia and Syria and to the head of the Jewish community in Baghdad; it was also used by scribes in the service of the Egyptian Mamlūk Sultanate to designate the Zaydī and Almohade "Caliphs" in the Yemen and North Africa, whose title to the Caliphate was not admitted. This meaning of pretender or false claimant is confirmed by an Arabic-Spanish vocabulary of 1505, which explains *za'īm as "hablador de sobervias, vanaglorioso.*"[9] The word *za'īm* came into general use in the 1930s, when an Arabic equivalent for *Duce* or *Führer* was required.

In all these, the new meaning is an extension rather than a replacement of the old political content, which still remains and can affect the use and understanding of these terms in Arab political life, often to the confusion of outside observers. In another type of loan-translation, the political meaning is wholly new. Thus, the word *inqilāb*, in classical Arabic, means revolution in the literal sense—that is, revolving, turning round. In Turkish, it became and for long remained the "good" word for revolution, used of revolutions of which the user approves; in Arabic on the other hand it has acquired a pejorative meaning and is used in a sense which might be translated by the French *coup* or German *Putsch*—English experience happily provides no suitable equivalent.[10]

There are many other words, previously non-political, which have acquired a new political significance, drawn from panoccidental usage. They include such terms as *ḥurriyya,* freedom;[11] *al-ra'y al-'āmm,* public opinion; *majlis nuwwāb,* chamber of deputies; *majlis shuyūkh,* Senate; *isti'mār,* colonization; *muḥāfiz,* conservative; *waṭan,* country, *patrie; intikhāb,* election; *ta'āyush,* coexistence; and *taṣā'ud,* escalation.

The emergence of the modern Arabic political vocabulary is an important aspect of the political and cultural life of the Islamic world. A careful study of its development is essential to the evaluation of texts and documents; an appreciation of the layers of content of the current language of politics can contribute greatly to the decipherment of political symbols and kennings and thus to the better understanding of political thought, purpose, and process.

Sources and Notes

Abbreviations

AIUON	Annali dell'Istituto Universitario Orientale di Napoli
ArO	Archiv Orientální
AÜdtcfd	Ankara Üniversitesi Dil ve Tarih-Coğrafya Fakültesi Dergisi
BIE	Bulletin de l'Institut D'Égypte
BIFAO	Bulletin de l'Institut Français d'Archéologie Orientale du Caire
BSOAS	Bulleting of the School of Oriental and African Studies
GAL	Geschichte der arabischen Litteratur
JAOS	Journal of the American Oriental Society
MTM	Millī Tetebbü'ler Mejmū'asi
RCEA	Répertoire chronologique d'Épigraphie arabe
RSO	Rivista degli studi orientali
THITM	Türk Hukuk ve İktisat Tarihi Mecmuasi
TOEM	Ta'rīkh-i 'Othmānī Enjümeni mejmū'asi
ZDMG	Zeitschrift der Deutschen Morgenländischen Gesellschaft

Sources

"Hukûmet and Devlet," *Belleten* 46 (1982), 415–421.

"Serbestiyet," *Journal of the Faculty of Economics of the University of Istanbul* 41 (1983), 47–52.

"Meşveret," *Tarih Enstitüsü Dergisi* 12 (1981–82), 775–782.

"Siyāsa," in *In Quest of an Islamic Humanism: Arabic and Islamic Studies in Memory of Mohamed al-Nowaihi*, ed. A.H. Green (Cairo: American University in Cairo Press, 1984), 3–14.

"Usurpers and Tyrants: Notes on Some Islamic Political Terms," in *Logos Islamikos: Studia Islamica in Honorem Georgii Michaelis Wickens*, ed. Roger M. Savory and Dionisius A. Agius (Toronto: Pontifical Institute of Mediaeval Studies, 1984), 259–267.

"On the Quietist and Activist Traditions in Islamic Political Writing," *Bulletin of the School of Oriental and African Studies* 49 (1986), 141–147.

"Malik," *Cahiers de Tunisie* 35 (1987), 101–109.

"The Regnal Titles of the First Abbasid Caliphs," in *Dr. Zakir Husain Presentation Volume* (New Delhi, 1968), 13–22.

"Daftar," *Encyclopedia of Islam*, 2nd ed., 2: 77–81.

"Dīwān-i Humāyūn," *Encyclopedia of Islam*, 2nd ed., 2: 337–339.

"D̲jumhūriyya," *Encyclopedia of Islam*, 2nd ed., 2: 594–595.

"On Modern Arabic Political Terms" published as "On Some Modern Arabic Political Terms" in *Orientalia Hispanica,* vol. 1, *Arabica-Islamica,* ed J. M. Barral. (Leiden: Brill, 1974), 465–71.

Notes

Notes to Chapter 1

1. *Avrupanın ahvaline dair risale,* in *Muntahabat-i asar-i Rıfat Paşa* (Istanbul, n.d.), p. 5.
2. See for example J.M. Landau, *A Word Count of Modern Arabic Prose,* (New York, 1959), p. 333; M. Brill and others, *The Basic Word List of the Arabic Daily Newspaper,* (Jerusalem, 1940), p. 21.
3. See for example Abu'l-Faraj al-Isfahānī, *Kitāb al-Aghānī.* (Cairo, 1345/1926–1927), xii, p. 134 "*fa-innaka qāḍin bi'l-ḥukūmati 'ālim*"- "you are a *qaḍi* skilled in the administration of justice." Other examples in *Aghānī*, xi, pp. 63, 165; Ibn Qutayba, *Uyūn al-Akhbār,* (Cairo, 1383/1963) i, p. 67; Jāḥiẓ, *Kitāb al-Tarbī' wa'l-Tadwīr,* ed. C. Pellat, (Damascus 1955), 1. 16, and in the verses cited in the classical Arabic lexica, e.g. *Lisān al-'Arab*, xiv, p. 95; xv, pp. 31, 177, 304, xvi, p. 41, *Tāj al-'Arūs,* ix, p. 68.
4. Ibn 'Abd Rabbihi, *Al-'Iqd al-Farīd*, (Cairo, 1953), i, p. 5.
5. Kâtib Çelebi, *Irşād al-ḥayārā ilā tārīh al-Yūnān wa'l- Rūm wa'l-Naṣārā,* ms. TTK library no. 19, no pagination. Other Ottoman examples in 'Ayn-i 'Ālī, *Ḳavānīn-i Āl-i Osmān*, (Istanbul 1280/1863–1864), pp. 29–30, on certain hereditary sanjaks, with a measure of political and financial autonomy, called *hukûmet;* Naima, v, p. 405; Raşid, i, p. 328.

6. Jabartī, *Muẓhir al-Taqdīs*, (Cairo, n.d.), ii, p. 91. Cf., the Turkish text of Bonaparte's letter to the governor of Egypt, published in Cevdet, *Tarih* (2nd edition, Istanbul 1309/1891–1892), vi, p. 405.
7. E.g. *Bonapart tarihi* (a Turkish translation of the first part of Carlo Botta's *Storia d'Italia* 1789–1815), (1st edition, Cairo 1249/1834, 2nd edition, Istanbul 1293/1876), i, pp. 4, 6, 10, 13, 16–17, 33; Cf. *Itḥāf al-Mulūk* (Arabic translation of William Robertson's *History of the Reign of Charles V*), (Būlāq, 1258/1842), passim.
8. Ms. in Egyptian National Library, History 435, translated by Father Anṭūn Rafā'īl Zākhūr. Cf. Jamāl al-Dīn al-Shayyāl, *Ta'rīkh al-Tarjama wa'l ḥaraka al-thaqāfiyya fī 'aṣr Muḥammad 'Alī* (Cairo, 1951), p. 216.
9. Rifā'a Rāfi' al-Ṭahṭāwī, *Takhlīṣ al-Ibrīz fī talkhīṣ Bārīz*, (1st edition Cairo, 1250/1834 eds. Mahdī 'Allām, Aḥmad Aḥmad Badawī and Anwar Lūqā, Cairo, n.d.? 1958), p. 142.
10. For Turkish examples, see *Tarih-i Cevdet*, i, pp. 17–20; for an Arabic discussion of the term and its meaning see Ḥusayn al-Marṣafī, *Al-Kalim al-thamān*, (Cairo, 1298/1881), pp. 30–35.
11. Polybius, *History*, vi, 9, x. For a discussion see Arthur Hatto, "'Revolution': an enquiry into the usefulness of an historical term" in *Mind*, lviii, (1949), pp. 495–517.
12. Ibn al-Muqaffa', *Risāla fī'l-Ṣaḥāba*, in Muḥammad Kurd 'Alī, ed., *Rasā'il al-Bulaghā'*, (4th edition, Cairo 1374/1954), p. 125; edited and translated into French by Charles Pellat, *Conseilleur du Calife*, (Paris, 1976), p. 38.

13. *Al-Adab al-Ṣaghīr*, in *Rasā'il al-Bulaghā'*, p. 17, *Al-Adab al-Kabīr wa'l-Adab al-Ṣaghīr*, (Beirut, 1956), p. 124.
14. *Rasā'īl, al-Bulaghā'*, p. 50; Beirut edition, p. 26.
15. Ṭabarī, *Tārīkh*, ii, p. 2009, Cf., *Kitāb al-Aghānī*, (Būlāq, 1285/1868–1869), xx, p. 104; Ibn 'Abd Rabbihi, *Al-'Iqd al-Farīd*, ii, p. 197.
16. Ṭabarī, iii, p. 86.
17. Ṭabarī, iii, p. 115.
18. Ṭabarī, iii, p. 96.
19. *Rasā'il Ikhwān al-Ṣafā* (Cairo, 1347/1928), i, pp. 130–131. Cf. i, p. 106; iii, p. 258; iv, pp. 234–237.

Notes to Chapter 2

1. The Turkish text of the Rescript is widely available. I have used the collection of documents edited by A. Şeref Gözübüyük and Suna Kili, *Türk Anayasa Metinleri* (Ankara, 1957), pp. 3–5.
2. A. Belin, "Charte des Turks" in *Journal Asiatique*, IIIe série, ix, (1840), p. 22, note 1. Belin was no doubt acquainted with the *Vocabulaire français-turc* published in Paris in 1831 by the French dragoman and orientalist T.X. Bianchi; under "Liberté" he has the following entry:
   LIBERTÉ, état d'une personne libre, ازادلق *azadliq*, ازادى *azadi*, سربستلك *serbestlik*, سربستيت serbestiiet, حرّية *hurriïet*;—délivrance, قورتلش *qourtoulich*, خلاص *khalas*, اعتاق *i'taq*, a., s.—Recouvrer la—, خلاص بولمق *khalas boulmaq*;—mettre en—, donner la—, ازادلق كشاد ويرمك *azadliq, kuchad virmek*, خلاص اطلاق اعتاق *khalas, itlaq, i'taq e*, a-t., صاليويرمك salyvirmek, v.

3. *Encyclopaedia of Islam*, 2nd edition, s.v. "Ḥurriyya."
4. Articles III of the Treaty. Italian text in G. F. de Martens, *Recueil de traités* iv, (Göttingen, 1795), pp. 610–612; Turkish text in *Mecmua-i muahedat*, iii, (Istanbul, 1297), pp. 255–257 and in *Tarih-i Cevdet*, 2nd edition, 1, (Istanbul, 1309), pp. 358–359. For an English version see J.C. Hurewitz, ed., *The Middle East and North Africa in World Politics, a Documentary Record*, 2nd edition, (New Haven and London), 1975, p. 94.
5. Yirmisekiz Mehmed Efendi, "Paris Sefaretnamesi" in *Kitabhane-i Ebüzziya*, (Istanbul, 1306), pp. 33–36, modern Turkish version, ed. Abdullah Uçman, in *Tercüman 1001 Temel Eser*, (Istanbul, n. d.), pp. 28 ff., contemporary French translation in Mehmed Efendi, *Le paradis des infidèles.. traduit de l'Ottoman par Julien-Claude Galland*, new edition by Gilles Veinstein, (Paris 1981), pp. 77–82.
6. *Icmal-i ahval-i Avrupa*, Süleymaniye Library, Esat Efendi no. 2062. For a description see V.L. Ménage, "Three Ottoman Treatises on Europe," in *Iran and Islam*, ed. C.E. Bosworth, (Edinburgh, 1971), pp. 425 ff.
7. Azmi Efendi, *Sefaretname*, in *Kitabhane-i Ebüzziya*, (Istanbul 1303), pp. 15–16.
8. "Moralı Esseyid Ali Efendi'nin Sefaretnamesi," in *Tarih-i Osmani Encümeni Mecmuası*, no. 23 (1329), pp. 1458, 1460, etc.
9. Cevdet, vi, pp. 280–281, 311, 395, 400. Cf. B. Lewis, *The Muslim Discovery of Europe*, (New York, 1982), pp. 52–53. For the reports of Hasan Paşa, the governor of the Morea, on these activities see Enver Ziya Karal, "Yunan Adalarının Fransızlar tarafindan işgalı ve Osmanlı-Rus münasebatı 1797–8," in *Tarih Semineri Dergisi*, I (1937), p. 113 ff.

10. Şanizade, *Tarih*, iv, (Istanbul, 1291), pp. 2–3.
11. A similar institution appears to have existed in Mamluk Egypt, where a certain type of grant (*iqṭā'*) accorded the right to all revenues, including those usually reserved for the Sultan's treasury. It is described by a term variously given as *darbastâ* and *karbastâ* in the Arabic sources. The word is not Arabic, and these forms may represent misreadings of an unfamiliar term by copyists and editors. See Hassanein Rabie, *The Financial System of Egypt A. H. 564–741/A. D. 1169–1341*, (London, 1972), pp. 43, 52, 57.

Notes to Chapter 3

1. See *Encyclopaedia of Islam,* 2nd edition, s. vv. "Madjlis" and "Mala'".
2. For examples of relevant hadith, see A. J. Wensinck and others, *Concordance de la tradition musulmane,* iii (Leiden, 1955), p. 212.
3. E.g. Zamakhsharī, *Kashshāf,* (Cairo 1373/1953), i, pp. 332–3, iv, p. 179; Fakhr al-Dīn Muḥammad ibn 'Umar al-Rāzī, *Mafātīḥ al-Ghayb*, (Cairo 1308/1890–1891), iii, p. 120.
4. 'Abd al-Ḥamīd, *Risāla.. fī naẓīḥat walī al-'ahd*, in Muḥammad Kurd 'Alī (ed), *Rasā'il al-Bulaghā'*, (Cairo, 1374/1953), p. 185; Ibn al-Muqaffa', *Ḥikam, ibid*, p. 155, Niẓām al-Mulk, *Siyāsatnāma*, chapter 18, "on having consultation with learned and experienced men," ed. and trans. Ch. Schefer, (Paris, 1891), text pp. 84–5, French translation, (Paris, 1893), pp. 124–6; English translation by H. Darke, (London, 1960), pp. 195–96.

5. H. A.R. Gibb in *Law in the Middle East*, edited by Majid Khadduri and H.J. Liebesny, (Washington, D.C., 1955), p. 16.
6. M. J. Kister, "Notes on an account of the Shūrā appointed by 'Umar b. al-Khaṭṭāb," in *Journal of Semitic Studies*, ix (1964), pp. 320–326.
7. For a somewhat idiosyncratic interpretation of the *wufūd* in the Umayyad period, see H. Lammens, *Études sur le règne du calife Omaiyade Mo'awia 1e*., (Beirut, 1906), pp. 59–64, 208.
8. Ibn Qutayba, *'Uyūn al -Akhbār*, (Cairo, 1383/1963), ii, p. 115.
9. Ibn Ḥazm, *Kitāb al-Milal wa'l-niḥal* (Cairo, 1964), iv, pp. 105–106 and 114–115.
10. *Ṣubḥ al-A'shā*, viii, (Cairo, 1335/1915), p.30.
11. Ibn Faḍlān, *Riḥla,* ed. Sāmī Dahhān, (Damascus, 1379/1959), pp. 91–92, French translation by M. Canard, *Annales de l'Institut d'Etudes Orientales,* xvi (1958), pp. 67–68.
12. See V. Minorsky, *Tadhkirat al-Mulūk,* (London, 1943), pp. 44, 53, 113 note 5, 120; G. Doerfer, *Türkische und Mongolische Elemente im Neupersischen,* i, (Wiesbaden, 1963), pp. 28–282; H.H. Zarinezade, *Fars dilinde Azerbaycan sözleri,* (Baku, 1962), pp. 248–250.
13. Ibn Kemal, *Tevarih-i Al-i Osman,* Defter, vii, ed. S. Turan (Ankara, 1957), p. 544.
14. D. Ayalon, "Studies on the Structure of the Mamluk Army—III," *Bulletin of the School of Oriental and African Studies,* xv (1954) p. 69; E. Tyan, *Institutions du Droit Public Musulman,* ii, (Paris-Beirut 1956), pp. 171–81; Qalqashandī, *Ṣubḥ,* vi, 28, xi, pp. 153–156; al-Maqrīzī, *Sulūk,* ed. M.M. Ziyada,

(Cairo, 1941), ii, pp. 64, 85–86, 182, 485, 551, 626, 634, 645, 746, 890, with an editorial note; idem, *Khiṭaṭ,* (ed. Būlāq) ii, p. 64; Abu'l-Maḥāsin, *Nujūm* (Cairo), x, p. 190.

15. Lutfi, *Tarih,* p. 21; Yazıcıoğlu Ali, *Selcuḳname,* cited in Agâh Sırrı Levend, *Turk Dilinde Gelişme ve Sadeleşme Safhaları,* (Ankara, 1949), p. 34.
16. Naima, i, pp. 131, 146, 155, 180, 273, 413, ii, pp. 354, 360, iii, p. 54, iv, pp. 298, 413, v, pp. 60, 203, 281–3; Kemalpaşazade, p. 127; Vasif, i, pp. 316–8, 221, 222, 274; Cevdet, ii, pp. 276 ff., iv, p. 289.
17. Şanizade, i, pp. 66, 73–75, 199–201, 365, iv, pp. 2–5, 201, 37 ff., 155–158, etc.
18. The text of the *Sened-i ittifāḳ* will be found in Şanizade, *Tarih*, i, pp. 66–78, and Cevdet, *Tarih*, ix, pp. 278–83. For accounts of the events leading to it, see, Şanizade, i, pp. 61 ff; Cevdet, ix, pp. 2 ff.; A. de Juchereau de Saint-Denys, *Révolutions de Constantinople en 1807 et 1808*, ii, (Paris, 1819), pp. 200 ff.; J.W. Zinkeisen, *Gesch. des osm. Reiches*, vii, Gotha 1863, pp. 564 ff; O. von Schlechta Wssehrd, *Die Revolutionen in Constantinopel in den Jahren 1807 und 1808*, in *SBAk. Wien* (1882), pp. 184–8. For studies and views of the pact see I.H. Uzunçarşılı, *Alemdar Mustafa Paşa*, (Istanbul, 1942), pp. 138–44; A.F. Miller, *Mustafa Pasha Bayraktar*, (Moscow, 1947), pp. 283–91; A. Selçuk Özçelik, "Senedi Ittifak," in *Istanbul Üniv. Hukuk Fak. Mec.*, xxiv (1959), pp. 1–12; T.Z. Tunaya, *Türkiyenin siyasi hayatında batılılaşma hareketleri*, (Istanbul, 1960), pp. 25–6; Ş. Mardin, *The Genesis of Young Ottoman Thought,* (Princeton, N.J., 1962), pp. 145–8.
19. *loc. cit.*

20. On Mahmud Raif, see Faik Reşit Unat, *Osmanlı Sefirleri ve Sefaretnameleri*, (Ankara, 1968), pp. 178–179; S. J. Shaw, *Between Old and New in the Ottoman Empire under Sultan Selim III 1789–1807*, (Cambridge, Mass., 1971), pp. 89, 449 n. 16, etc. Part of Mahmud Raif's description was published by Gilles Veinstein, in Mehmed Efendi, *Le paradis des infidèles*, (Paris, 1981), pp. 242–248.
21. *Bonapart Tarihi nam-i diger Italya Tarihi*, (Istanbul, 1293/1876), i, pp. 5 ff.
22. *Takhlīṣ al-ibrīz fī talkhīṣ Bārīz*, ed. Mahdī 'Allām et al. (Cairo n.d.), chapter 3, pp. 138–143.

Notes to Chapter 4

1. See al-Tahānawī, *Kashshāf iṣṭilāḥāt al-funūn* (Calcutta, 1862), pp. 664–65; Ibn Sīda, *Kitāb al-Mukhaṣṣaṣ fī 'l-lugha*, ed. M. Ṭālbī (Tunis, 1956), p. 162. The so-called *siyāsījān* of Sassanid Armenia are probably the result of a misreading; see J. H. Kramers, "The Military Colonization of the Caucasus and Armenia under the Sassanids," *Bulletin of the School of Oriental and African Studies*, Vol. 8 (1936), pp. 613–18; A. Christensen, *L 'Iran sous les Sassanides* (Copenhagen, 1944), p. 369.
2. 'Abd al-Ḥamīd al-Kātib, *Risāla ilā 'l-kuttāb* in A. Z. Ṣafwat (ed.), *Jamharat rasā'il al-'arab,* (Cairo, 1356/1937), II, pp. 534–40; also in M. Kurd 'Alī (ed.), *Rasā'il al-bulaghā'* (Cairo, 1946), p. 223; translated in B. Lewis, *Islam from the Prophet Muhammad to the Capture of Constantinople* (New York, 1974), I, p. 189; Cf. al-Jahshiyārī, *Kitāb al-Wuzarā' wa'l-kuttāb,* ed. Muṣṭafā al-Saqqā' (Cairo 1357/1938), p. 75;

Ibn Khaldūn, *al-Muqaddima* (Beirut, 1900), II, p. 28; Franz Rosenthal, *The Muqaddima: an Introduction to History* (New York, 1958), II, pp. 32–33; al-Qalqashandī, *Ṣubḥ al-a'shā* (Cairo, 1331/1913–1337/1918), I, p. 97.

3. Al-Balādhurī, *Futūḥ al-buldān,* ed. M. J. de Goeje (Leiden, 1866), p. 279; Cf. al-Ṭabarī, *Ta'rīkh al-rusul wa'l-mulūk,* ed. M. J. de Goeje *et al.* (Leiden, 1879–1901), I, pp. 2776–7.
4. "Ḥusn siyāsatika," Ibn 'Abd al-Ḥakam, *Futūḥ miṣr wa akhbāruhā,* ed. C. C. Torrey (New Haven, 1922), p. 160.
5. Ibn 'Abd Rabbihi, *al-'Iqd al-farīd,* ed. Muḥammad Sa'īd al-'Iryān (Cairo, 1372/1953) II, p. 278; Cf. al-Ṭabarī, *Ta'rīkh,* II, p. 75; Cf. J. Wellhausen, *The Arab Kingdom and its Fall* (Calcutta, 1972), p. 123.
6. Al-Ṭabarī, *Ta'rīkh,* II, p. 1662.
7. *"Siyāsatukum," ibid.*, II, p. 1788.
8. R. E. Geyer, *Altarabische Diiamben* (Leipzig, 1908), p. 5.
9. *"Li-marḍī al-siyāsati al-hāshimī,"* Kumayt, *al-Hāshimiyāt,* ed. J. Horovitz (Leiden, 1904), p. 154.
10. Al-Balādhurī, *Ansāb al-ashrāf,* ed. S. D. F. Goitein (Jerusalem, 1936), V, p. 207.
11. Al-Balādhurī, *Ansāb,* ed. Muḥammad Ḥamidullah (Cairo, 1959), I, p. 504.
12. Hilāl al-Sābī, *Kitāb al-wuzarā',* ed. H. F. Amedroz (Leiden, 1904), p. 347; Cf. D. Sourdel, *Le Vizirat Abbaside* (Damascus, 1960), p. 568.
13. Ibn Qutayba, *'Uyūn al-akhbār* (Cairo, 1963 ff), I, p. 25.
14. *Ibid.*
15. Al-Ṭabarī, *Ta'rīkh,* III, p. 29.

16. Al-Mas'ūdī, *Murūj al-dhahab,* ed. C. Barbier de Meynard (Paris, 1861–1877), VI, p. 221; al-Ya'qūbī, *Kitāb al-buldān,* ed. M.J. de Goeje (Leiden, 1892), II, p. 474; Cf. *Murūj,* VI, p. 223, "*wa lahu khuṭab wa mawā'iẓ wa siyar wa siyāsat al-mulk*"; Cf. *idem, Kitāb al-tanbīh,* ed. M.J. de Goeje (Leiden, 1894), p. 342, "he governs (*yasūsu*) with the government (*siyāsa*) of kings and pounces with the pounce of a lion."
17. Al-Mas'ūdī, *Tanbīh,* p. 346; Cf. however the passages quoted by al-Ṭabarī, *Ta'rīkh,* III, pp. 653, 704.
18. *"Al-'ilm bi'l-siyāsa"* and *"Maḥmūd al-siyāsa"* in Ibn Ṭayfūr, *Kitāb Baghdād,* ed., Muḥammad Zāhid Ibn al-Ḥasan al-Kawtharī (Cairo, 1949), pp. 31, 32; repeated in Ibn Khaldūn, *al-Muqaddima,* II, p. 151.
19. "*Al-'ibād yasūsuhum ibnāki,*" *Murūj,* VI, p. 269.
20. *Ibid.*, VI, p. 282–3.
21. *Rasā'il al-bulaghā'*, p. 129; C. Pellat, *Conseilleur de calife, Ibn al-Muqaffa'*, (Paris, 1976), p. 51.
22. J. Schacht, *The Origins of Muhammadan Jurisprudence* (Oxford, 1950), pp. 58–9; Cf. *ibid.*, pp. 95, 102; *Risāla fi'l-ṣaḥāba* in *Rasā'il al-bulaghā',* pp. 125 ff; also in C. Pellat, *Ibn al-Muqaffa'*, pp. 39 ff.
23. *Ṣaḥāba* in *Rasā'il al-bulaghā',* p. 129; also in C. Pellat, *Conseilleur de calife,* p. 29; Cf. S.D.F. Goitein, "A Turning Point in the History of the Muslim State," *Islamic Culture,* vol. 23 (1949), p. 120 ff; *idem, Studies in Islamic History and Institutions* (Leiden, 1966), p. 149 ff; E. I. J. Rosenthal, *Political Thought in Medieval Islam, an Introductory Outline* (Cambridge, 1958), p. 71 ff; Cf. Ibn Khaldūn, *Kitāb al-'Ibar* (Būlāq, 1284/1867), V, p. 478, concerning the right of the ruler to make laws.

24. See for example his *Rasā'il,* ed. 'Abd al-Salām Hārūn (Cairo, 1965), I, pp. 99, 102; also *Rasā'il,* ed. Ḥasan al-Sandūbī (Cairo, 1352/1933), p. 126 also *al-Bayān wa'l-tabyīn,* ed. 'Abd al-Salām Hārūn (Cairo, 1380/1940), III. p. 366 ff, and IV, p. 30.
25. Hilāl al-Ṣābī', *Kitāb al-Wuzarā',* pp. 64, 69; Cf. A. Mez, *Die Renaissance des Islams* (Heidelberg, 1922), pp. 88–89, English translation (London, 1937), pp. 97–98.
26. Ibn 'Abd Rabbihi, *al-'Iqd,* I, p. 18.
27. Al-Jāḥiẓ, *Rasā'il,* ed. 'Abd al-Salām Hārūn, I, p. 99; cf. *ibid.,* I, p. 102; *al-Bayān,* IV, p. 30.
28. Cf. A.F. L. Beeston, *The Arabic language Today* (London, 1970), p. 112 ff.
29. Ibn al-Sirafī, quoted by Frithiof Rundgren in *Donum Natalicum H.S. Nyberg Oblatum* (Upsala, 1954), p. 136.
30. Al-Tawḥīdī, *Kitāb al-Imtā' wa'l-mu'ānasa* (Cairo, 1939–44), II, p. 32.
31. On *siyāsa* as political philosophy, see Mas'ūdī, *Murūj,* II, p. 209; III, pp. 82–3, 439; IV, pp. 7–16 on his own (lost) book on this subject. The word *siyāsa* occurs in book titles of the third/ninth century: *Siyāsat al-nafs* ascribed to al-Qāsim b. Ibrāhīm al-Ḥasanī (d. 246/860), C. Brockelmann, *GAL,* GI, p. 186; *Kitāb al-siyāsa fī tadbīr al-ri'āsa,* a *Fürstenspiegel* attributed to Aristotle for the guidance of Alexander and allegedly translated into Arabic by Yaḥyā (Yuḥ-anna) ibn Biṭrīq, *GAL,* GI, p. 203, SI, p. 364; *Kitāb al-imāma wa'l-siyāsa,* attributed to Ibn Qutayba; it is not by Ibn Qutayba but is probably contemporaneous, see de Goeje, "*Kitāb al-imāma wa-'s-siyāsa* par Abou Muhammad Abdallah ibn Qotaiba," *Rivista*

degli Studi Orientali, Vol. I (1907), pp. 415–21, also *GAL* SI, p. 187. In all these titles, *siyāsa* probably means statecraft. In al-Fārābī it has clearly acquired the technical sense of the word 'politics' among the Greek philosophers.

32. *Al-Fakhrī* (Cairo, 1317 A.H.), pp. 20–21; H. Derenbourg (ed.), *Bibliothèque de l'École des Haute Études,* fac. 25 (Paris, 1895), p. 30; E. Amar, *al-Fakhri–Histoire des Dynasties musulmanes,* French translation (Paris, 1910), p. 37; C.E.J. Whitting, *al-Fakhri: On the Systems of Government and the Mohammadan Dynasties,* English translation (London, 1947), p. 20.
33. *Faraj* (Cairo & Baghdad, 1375/1955), pp. 241–2; translated by A.F.L. Beeston, "The Genesis of the *Maqamāt* Genre," *Journal of Arabic Literature,* Vol. 2 (1971), p. 4.
34. *Rāḥat al-ṣudūr,* ed. Muhammad Iqbal (London, 1921), p. 97; A.K.S. Lambton, "Ḥādjib," *Encyclopedia of Islam,* 2nd ed., III, p. 147a; but also compare *Rāḥat al-ṣudūr,* p. 118, where the word is clearly used in the older meaning, "*man ḥasunat siyāsatuhu dāmat ri'āsatuhu.*"
35. *Qābūsnāma,* ed. R. Levy (London, 1951), p. 130; English translation by Levy, (London, 1951), p. 233.
36. *Kitāb al-Aḥkām al-Sulṭāniyya,* ed. R. Enger (Bonn, 1853), p. 375; (Cairo, n.d.). p. 211; E. Fagnan, *Les statuts governementaux ou régles de droit public et administratif* (Algiers, 1915), p. 469. In the parallel text of Abū Ya'lā, ed. Muḥammad Amīn 'Umrān (Cairo, 1357 A.H.), p. 240, the word is significantly missing.

37. Abū Shāma, *Kitāb al-rawḍatayn fī akhbār al-dawlatayn* (1st ed.), I, pp. 6, 7, 11, 13; (2nd ed), ed. M. Ḥilmī Aḥmad (Cairo,1962), I, p.32; Cf. *ibid.* (1st ed.), I, p. 219, (2nd ed.), I, p. 560. Poliak interpreted this as a reference to the *yasa,* the Mongol code and was challenged on this point by V. Minorsky; see A. N. Poliak, "The influence of Chingiz Khan's *Yasa* upon the Organization of the Mamlūk State," *Bulletin of the School of Oriental and African Studies,* vol. 10 (1942), pp. 863, 875.
38. *Rawḍatayn* (1st ed.), I, p. 219; (2nd ed.), I, p. 560.
39. For example, the Seljuk Sultan Sanjar, in a letter to the caliph, speaks of "*siyâseti cumhûr*" as one of the duties of the sovereign. Quoted in Mehmed Köymen, *Büyük Selçuklu Imparatorluğu Tarihi* (Ankara, 1954), p. 223.
40. Ibn Taghrī Birdī, *al-Nujūm al-Zāhira* (Cairo, 1348/1929 ff), VI, pp. 268–9 and VII, pp. 182–7. Cf. D. Ayalon, "Studies on the Structure of the Mamluk Army: III," *Bulletin of the School of Oriental and African Studies,* vol. 15 (1953), p. 68; al-Maqrīzī, *al-Mawā'iz wa'l-I'tibār bi-dhikr al-khiṭaṭ wa'l-āthār* (Būlāq, 1854), II, pp. 219–22, 306; Cf. *Nujūm* (Cairo), VII, pp. 182–87; A. N. Poliak, "Le caractère coloniale de l'Etat mamelouk dans ses rapports avec la Horde d'Or," *Revue des études islamiques,* vol. 9 (1935) p. 235, *idem,* "Chingiz Khan's *Yasa,*"*op cit., p. 862 ff;* H. Laoust, *Essai sur les doctrines socials et politiques de Taki-d-Din Ahmad b. Taimiyya* (Cairo, 1939), p. 55; and note V. V. Barthold, *Turkistan down to the Mongol Invasions* (London, 1968), pp. 41–42.
41. Laoust, *op cit.,* p. 55ff; also see Ibn Qayyim al-Jawziyya, *al-Ṭuruq al-ḥukumiyya,* ed. Muḥammad

Jamal (Cairo, 1961) and Ibn Taymiyya, *al-Siyāsa al-shar'iyya,* ed. Muḥammad 'Abd Allah al-Sammān (Cairo, 1381/1961).

42. *Al-Muqaddima* (Beirut, 1900), p. 302; Rosenthal, *The Muqaddima,* III, p. 37 ff; de Slane, *Les Prolégomenes* (Paris, 1863–68), II, p. 126 ff.
43. D. Santillana, *Instituzioni di diritto musulmano malichita* (Rome, 1926), II, p. 561, citing Ibn Farhūn.
44. Rifā'a al-Ṭahṭāwī, *Takhlīṣ al-ibrīz fi talkhīṣ bārīz* (Cairo, 1958), pp. 138, 142–9.
45. E. Z. Karal, "Yavuz Sultan Selimin oğlu Şehzade Süleyman'a Manisa sancağini idare etmesi için gönderdiği siyasetnâme," *Belleten,* vol. 6 (1942), pp. 37–44; Cf. U. Heyd, *"Djazā," Encyclopedia of Islam* (2nd. ed.), III pp. 518b–519b, for examples in Ottoman legal documents, see B. Durdev et al., *Kanun i Kanun-Name* (Sarajevo, 1957). *passim.*
46. Na'īmā *Ta'rīkh,* I, p. 288.
47. Abdulbaki Golpinarlı, "Hurûfilik ve Mir-i 'Alem Celāl Bik'in bir Mektubu," *Türkiyat Mecmuasi,* Vol. 14 (Istanbul, 1964), p. 109.
48. Cevdet, *Tarih-i Cevdet* (Istanbul, A.H. 1301–1309), IX, p. 171.

Notes to Chapter 5

1. For a brief but interesting recent discussion of these traditions, see R. Stephen Humphreys, "The political values of traditional Islam and their role in twentieth-century Egypt" in *Self-views in Historical Perspective in Egypt and Israel*, ed. Shimon Shamir (Tel-Aviv, 1981), pp. 25–32.

2. Ṭabarī, *Ta'rīkh*, 1: 2053; Cf. ibid., 1: 2020; Abū Yūsuf, *Kitāb al-Kharāj* (Cairo, 1382/1962–1963), p. 85; Abū 'Ubayd al-Qāsim ibn Sallām, *Kitāb al-Amwāl*, ed. Muḥammad Ḥāmid al-Fīqī (Cairo, 1353/1934), p. 34. Similar expressions occur in other early letters ascribed to Muslim leaders. See for example the texts collected by Muḥammad Ḥamīdullah, *Majmū'at al-wathā'iq al-siyāsīya* (Cairo, 1376/1956), especially pp. 295 ff.
3. References in A. J. Wensinck, *A Handbook of early Muhammadan Tradition* (Leiden, 1921), p. 43 and idem., *Concordance*, 5: 179–180. See further D. B. Macdonald. *The Religious Attitude and Life in Islam* (Chicago, 1909), p. 243; idem, "Fiṭra," *EI*², 2: 931–932.
4. Qur'ān, 18: 28 and 26: 150–152; Cf. 28: 3/4–5/6, 34: 33/34–37/38, and 59: 7. For traditions, see A. J. Wensinck, *Concordance*, Svv. "*Ma'ṣiya*," "*ẓulm*," etc.
5. Qur'ān, 4: 59, Traditions in al-Muttaqī, *Kanz al-'ummāl* (Hyderabad, 1312), 3: 197 ff. Further examples in Wensinck, *Concordance*, Svv. "*imām*," "*amīr*," "*wālī*," etc.
6. This development was first traced and analysed by A. von Kremer (*Geschichte der herrschenden des Ideen Islams* [Leipzig, 1868], pp. 413 ff. and *Culturgeschichte des Orients unter den Chalifen* [Vienna, 1875], 1: 380 ff) and presented in exemplary form by David Santillana, *Istituzioni di diritto musulmano malichita con riguardo anche al sistema sciafiita* (Rome, 1926), vol. 1 especially pp. 12–24, where the major Arabic sources are cited. See further H. A. R. Gibb, *Studies on the Civilization of Islam* (London, 1962), pp. 141 ff;

idem, "Constitutional Organization" in *Law in the Middle East,* ed. Majid Khadduri and Herbert J. Liebesny (Washington, D.C., 1955), 1: 3–27. The whole question has recently been thoroughly and comprehensively reexamined by Ann K. S. Lambton in a major work, *State and Government in Medieval Islam* (London, 1981).

7. On this and other terms used in the Qur'ān, see Toshihiko Izutsu, *Ethico-religious Concepts in the Qur'ān* (Montreal, 1966).
8. Ṭabarī, *Ta'rīkh*, 3: 197.
9. E.g., Kulīnī. *Uṣūl*, pp. 4, 63.
10. Qalqashandī, *Ṣubḥ al-a'shā* (Cairo, 1334/1915), 8: 29 and 51–52: Shihāb al-Dīn al-'Umarī, *Al-ta'rīf bi'l-muṣṭalaḥ al-sharīf* (Cairo, 1312), pp. 55–56. Maqrīzī, in the *Khiṭaṭ* (ed. Wiet; 3: 297) refers to the Christian ruler of Nubia as *mutamallik*, but elsewhere (e.g., *Sulūk*, 1: 611) discussing the same episode, follows the normal practice of according this old established monarchy the title *malik.*
11. Santillana, 1: 24.
12. Lambton, pp. 74 ff.
13. See, for example, al-Ghazālī, *Al-Iqtiṣād fī 'l-I'tiqād* (Cairo, n.d.), pp. 102–108: "We do not concede this voluntarily, but necessity may make licit that which is forbidden. Thus, we know that to eat carrion is forbidden, but to starve to death is worse." In the same way, Ghazālī argues, a tyrannical ruler who validates the law and thus maintains the life of the community is better than none at all and the resulting communal death.
14. Wansharīsī's *fatwā* was included in his *al-Mi'yār al-Mughrib* (Fez, 1896–1897), 2: 90–106 and

published in a critical edition by Ḥusayn Mu'nis, "Asnā 'l-matājir fī bayān man ghalaba 'alā watanihi 'l-Nasārà wa-lam yuhājir," in *Revista del Instituto de Estudios Islamicos en Madrid*, 5 (1957), Arabic section pp. 129–191, summary in Spanish section pp. 273–275. On the problem of emigration from Muslim lands conquered by non-Muslims, see in general Santillana, 1: 69–72, where other sources are cited.

15. Ibn Mājah, *Sunan* (Cairo, 1372/1952), 2: 1366–1367.
16. Ibn al-Athīr, *Usd al-ghāba* (Cairo, 1285–1287/1869–1871), 5: 155.
17. E.g., Ibn Sīda, *al-Mukhaṣṣaṣ* (Cairo, 1316–1321), 12: 250.
18. Abū Shāma, *Tarājim rijāl al-qarnayn al-sādis wa'l-sābi'*, ed. Muḥammad Zāhid al-Kawtharī (Cairo, 1366/1947), p. 81; Ibn al-'Adīm, "Biography of Rāšid al-Dīn Sinān," ed. B. Lewis, in *Arabica*, 13 (1966), 266; Ibn al-Fuwaṭī, *Al-Ḥawādith al-jāmi'a*, ed. Muṣṭafà Jawād (Baghdad, 1951), p. 218; Qalqashandī, *Ṣubḥ*, 6: 513. See further Ḥasan al-Bāshā, *Al-Alqāb al-Islāmīya* (Cairo, 1957), pp. 310–311.

Notes to Chapter 6

1. Abū 'Abdallāh 'Ubaydallāh ibn Muḥammad ibn Baṭṭa, *Kitāb al-Sharḥ wa'l-Ibāna 'alā uṣūl al-Sunna wa'l-Diyāna*, ed. H. Laoust (Damascus, 1958), 66ff.
2. For further references to this *ḥadīth*, see A.J. Wensinck (ed.), *Concordance et indices de la tradition musulmane* (Leiden, 1936–1969), I, 327. Goldziher, in a rare error, attributes this *ḥadith* to the Kharijites and sees in it an expression of

Kharijite egalitarianism: *Vorlesungen über den Islam* (Heidelberg, 1910), 205; English translation, *Introduction to Islamic Theology and Law* (Princeton, N.J., 1981), 171, and additional note e. But as S. D. Goitein showed, *Studies in Islamic History and Institutions* (Leiden, 1966), 203–4, it was already used by Abū Yūsuf, in a volume dedicated to the Caliph, as an argument in favor of unquestioning submission to authority.

3. See Ann K. S. Lambton, *State and Government in Medieval Islam* (Oxford, 1981), 43–68; Tilman Nagel, *Staat und Glaubensgemeinschaft im Islam* 1 (Zurich and Munich, 1981), passim, espec. pp. 153 ff.; Goitein, *Studies,* 149–167.
4. *loc. cit.*
5. Badr al-Dīn Muḥammad ibn Ibrāhīm ibn Jamāʻa, *Taḥrīr al-Aḥkām fī Tadbīr Ahl al-Islām,* ed. H. Kofler in *Islamica,* VI, 1934, 357. For discussions of this passage, see Lambton, *State and Government,* 138–43; H. A. R. Gibb and H. Bowen, *Islamic Society and the West,* i/I (London, 1950), 32; D. Santillana, *Istituzioni di diritto musulmano malichita* (Rome, 1926), I, 24; Alfred von Kremer, *Geschichte der herrschenden Ideen des Islams,* (Leipzig, 1868), 416.
6. For examples, with Jewish and Christian parallels, see A. J. Wensinck, "The refused dignity," in *A Volume of Oriental Studies presented to Edward G. Browne* (Cambridge, 1922), 491–9.
7. See Lambton, *State and Government,* 107–8; Henri Laoust, *La politique de Ǧazālī* (Paris, 1970), 90 ff.
8. On the termination of the contract of allegiance to a Caliph, see E. Tyan, *Institutions du droit public musulman* (Paris, 1953), I, 357–61; II, (Paris, 1956),

366–8; Henri Laoust, *Essai sur les doctrines sociales et politiques de Taki-d-Dīn Aḥmad b. Taimīya* (Cairo, 1939), 313–15; Lambton, *State and Government,* 74–5 (on Bāqillānī), etc.

9. See for example the major article by Laura Veccia Vaglieri, "Il conflitto 'Alī-Mu'āwiya e la secessione kharigita riesaminati alla luce di fonti ibadite," *AIUON*, 1952, 1–94; idem, 'Traduzione de passi riguardanti il conflitto 'Alī-Mu'āwiya e la secessione kharigita', *AIUON*, 1953, 1–98; Muḥammad Kafāfī, 'The rise of kharijism according to Abū Sa'id Muḥammad ... al-Qalhātī," *Bulletin of the Faculty of Arts (Cairo),* XIV, 1952, 29–48; Erling Ladewig Petersen, *'Ali and Mu'awiya in Early Arabic Tradition*, second edition (Odense, 1974).
10. See Said Amir Arjomand, *The Shadow of God and the Hidden Imam: religion, political order and societal changes in Shi'ite Iran from the beginning to 1890* (Chicago, 1984), 58–9. For some sayings of the Imām 'Alī al-Riḍā, see al-Ya'qūbī, *Ta'rīkh* (Beirut, 1960), II, 453–4.
11. See especially the writings of 'Abd al-'Azīz al-Dūrī, "Daw' jadīd 'alā 'l-da'wa al-'Abbāsiyya," in *Majallat kulliyyat al-ādāb wa'l-funūn,* II, Baghdad, 1957, 64–82, and his edition of the *Akhbār al-Dawla al-'Abbāsiyya* (Beirut, 1971); Farouk 'Omar, *The Abbasid Caliphate 132/750–170/786* (Baghdad, 1969); idem, "Aspects of Abbasid Husaynid relations," *Arabica* 22, 1976, 170–79; idem, *Al-'Abbāsiyyūn al-awā'il 132–70/750–86,* 2 vols. (Beirut, 1390/1970); Moshe Sharon, *Black Banners from the East: the establishment of the 'Abbasid state; incubation of a revolt* (Jerusalem, 1983); idem, "The Abbasid *da'wa*

re-examined on the basis of the discovery of a new source," in *Arabic and Islamic Studies* (Bar-Ilan University, 1973), pp. xxi-xli; Jacob Lassner, *The Shaping of 'Abbasid rule* (Princeton N.J., 1980).

12. Abū Ja'far Muḥammad ibn Jarīr al-Ṭabarī, *Ta'rīkh al-Rusul wa'l-Mulūk,* ed. M.G. de Goeje and others (Leiden, 1879–1901), II, 1687–8.
13. Abū Muḥammad 'Abdallāh ibn Muslim ibn Qutayba, *'Uyūn al-Akhbār,* ed. Aḥmad Zakī al-'Adawī (Cairo 1343–1348/1925–1930), II, 115. The saying is attributed to a certain Sudayf, a mawla of the Banū Hāshim, who joined the revolt of Muḥammad ibn 'Abdallāh against al-Manṣūr in 145/762. The passage caught the attention of historians, and is quoted in several other places. See for example Ibn Qutayba, *Kitāb al-Shi'r wa'l-Shu'arā',* ed. M.J. Goeje (Leiden, 1904) 419; Ibn Abd Rabbihi, *Al-'Iqd al-Farīd,* II (Cairo, 1940), 32; Abū'l-Faraj al-Iṣfahānī, *Kitāb al-Aghānī,* XIV (Būlāq, 1285), 162. For a discussion of the context of this saying see Farouk Omar, *The Abbasid Caliphate,* 233–34.
14. 'Amr ibn Baḥr al-Jāḥiẓ, *Rasā'il,* ed. Ḥasan al-Sandūbī (Cairo, 1352/1933), 295.
15. An earlier version of parts of this paper was included in a larger study presented to a colloqium at UNESCO in December 1982.

Notes to Chapter 7

Bibliographical note: The numismatic and epigraphic evidence on the use of *Malik* in medieval Islamic states was reviewed and analysed by Ḥasan al-Bāshā, *Al-Alqāb al-Islāmiyya fi'l-ta'rīkh wa'l-wathā'iq wa'l-āthār,* (Cairo, 1957), pp. 496–506, and idem, *Al-Funūn al Islāmiyya wa'l-waẓā'if 'alā al-āthār al-'Arabiyya,* iii. (Cairo, 1966), pp. 1139–1142. The literary evidence relating to pre-Islamic Arabia was examined by Emile Tyan, *Institutions du droit public musulman,* I, *Le Califat,* (Paris, 1954), pp. 75–84, and Francesco Gabrieli, "Tribu e Stato nell'antica poesia araba" in his *L'Islam nella storia,* (Bari, 1966), pp. 9–26. The reappearance of monarchical titles and their use by Muslim rulers have been studied by Wilferd Madelung, "The Assumption of the title Shahanshah by the Buyids" and "The Reign of the Daylam (*Dawlat al-Daylam*)," in *Journal of Near Eastern Studies,* xxviii (1969), pp. 84–108 and 168–183, and by C.E. Bosworth, "The titulature of the early Ghaznavids," in *Oriens,* xv (1962), pp. 210–233. The revival and use of the term in the 19th and 20th centuries was studied by Ami Ayalon, "*Malik* in modern Middle Eastern Titulature," in *Die Welt des Islams,* xxiii-xxiv (1984), pp. 306–319.

1. *The diwans of 'Abīd b. al-Abraṣ and 'Āmir b. al-Ṭufail,* ed. and tr. Sir Charles Lyall, (Leiden, 1913), p. 64; text, p. 81.
2. *RCEA, (Repertoire Chronologique d'Épigraphie Arabe),* i, (Cairo, 1931), n. 1.
3. Ṭabarī, *Ta'rīkh al-Rusul wa'l-Mulūk,* i, p. 2754.
4. Al-Jāḥiẓ, *Rasā'il,* ed. Ḥasan al-Sandūbī, (Cairo, 1933), p. 117, French translation by Charles Pellat, in *AIEO*, x, (1952), p. 314.
5. Al-Bāshā, *Alqāb,* p. 497, citing *Inventaire des Monnaies des Khalifes Orientaux,* (St. Petersburgh, 1877), p. 123.

6. Al-Bāshā, *Alqāb,* p. 497, citing *Inventaire,* p. 135.
7. Cf. Madelung, op.cit.
8. Al-Bāshā, *Alqāb,* p. 505, citing Ibn al-Athīr, ix, p. 171.
9. Ibid., citing *RCEA*, vi, no. 2177, vii, no. 2577 and 2760, and al-Maqrīzī, *Sulūk*, i, p. 168. See al-Qalqashandī, *Ṣubḥ al-A'shā*, vi, p. 16.
10. Idem, p. 502, citing *RCEA*, vi, no. 2378; vii, no. 2734; al-Qalqashandī, *Ṣubḥ al-A'shā*, v, p. 455.
11. Al-Bāshā, *Alqāb*, p. 503, citing *RCEA*, xi, no. 4308.
12. Idem, pp. 504–505, citing *RCEA*, xii, no. 4554 and vii, no. 2707.
13. Idem, p. 503, citing *RCEA,* x, no. 3735; *RCEA,* ix, no. 3509; and *RCEA,* xi, no. 3272. For some other territorial titles, al-Bāshā, *Funūn, loc. cit.*
14. Bosworth, "Titulature … ," p. 221.
15. See further Bernard Lewis, *The Muslim Discovery of Europe,* (New York and London, 1982), pp. 203–205.

Notes to Chapter 8

1. Sometimes, on his accession, the new Caliph abandons the title which he used as heir apparent, and adopts a new one. Given the archaising tendency found in many Muslim historians, it is not surprising that some of them should have ascribed the practice of adopting regnal titles to the Umayyads and even to the patriarchal Caliphs; some even adduce lists of Umayyad titles, usually rather unflattering. These are quite fictitious, as was realized by some of the classical Muslim historians (e.g. Mas'ūdī, K. *al-Tanbīh wa'l-ishrāf,* Cairo 1354/1938, 289–90; French translation by Carra de Vaux, *Le livre de l'avertissement et de*

la revision, Paris 1897, 431–3; Khuwārizmī, *Mafātīḥ al-'ulūm*, Cairo n.d., 66. On the whole question see Hilāl al-Ṣābī, *Rusūm Dār al-Khilāfa*, ed. Mikhā'īl 'Awaḍ, Baghdad 1964, 128 ff; Qalqashandī, *Ma'āthir al-ināfa fī ma'ālim al-khilāfa*, ed. 'Abd al-Sattār Aḥmad Farrāj, i, Kuwait 1964, 20 ff.; idem, *Ṣubḥ al-a'shá*, v, Cairo 1333/1915, 477 ff.; E. Tyan, *Institutions du droit public musulman, i, Le califat*, Paris 1954, 483–8; A. Abel, 'Le Khalife presence sacrée,' in *Studia Islamica*, vii (1957), 29–45, especially 39 f.

2. G. van Vloten, *De Opkomst der Abbasiden in Chorasan*, Leiden, 1890, especially 132–40; idem, *Recherches sur la domination arabe, le Chiitisme et les croyances messianiques sous le Khalifat des Omayades,* Amsterdam 1894, 54 ff.; idem, "Zur Abbasidengeschichte," in *ZDMG*, lii (1898), 213–26 Cf. I. Goldziher, *Muhammedanische Studien,* ii, Halle 1890, 125–30.
3. One of the best-known ḥadiths of messianic content. See for example Ibn al-Athīr, *Usd al-ghāba,* v, Cairo 1280, 155.
4. On these writings see D.B. MacDonald, "Malāḥim," in *Enc. Islam,* 1st ed. and T. Fahd, "Djafr," in *Enc. Islam,* 2nd ed., where further references are given. Other studies include A. Abel, "Changements politiques et litterature eschatologique dans le monde musulman," in *Studia Islamica,* ii (1954), 23–43; idem, "L'Apocalypse de Bahira et la notion islamique du Mahdi," in *Annuaire de l'Institut de philologie et d'histoire orientales,* iii (1935), 1–12; B. Lewis, "An apocalyptic vision of Islamic history," in *BSOAS,* xiii (1950), 308–38; J. Bignami-Odier and G. Levi Della Vida, "Une version latine de l'apocalypse syro-arabe

de Serge-Bahira," in *Melanges d'Archeologie et d'histoire,* Ecole Francaise de Rome, 1950, 125–48.

5. N. Cohn, *The Pursuit of the Millennium,* London 1957, 20.
6. Cohn 21 ff, and passim.
7. On the revolt of Mukhtār see K.A. Fariq, "The story of an Arab diplomat," in *Studies in Islam,* iii (1966), 53–80, 119–42, 227–41; iv (1967), 50–59; earlier work in G. Levi Della Vida, "Mukhtār," in *Enc. Islam,* 1st ed.
8. On the history of Muslim messianism see C. Snouck Hurgronje, *Verspreide Geschriften,* i, Bonn-Leipzig 1923, 145–81; D.B. MacDonald, "al-Mahdī," in *Enc. Islam,* 1st ed; D.S. Margoliouth, "Mahdi," in *Hasting's Enc. of Religion and Ethics,* and, including more recent developments, E. Sarkisyanz, *Russland und der Messianismus des Orients.* Tubingen 1955, 223–96.
9. On the use of the term *Qā'im* among the Isma'ilis, see W. Ivanow, *Ismaili Tradition concerning the Rise of the Fatimids,* London 1942, 50 ff. and index.
10. For a recent survey of the problems and literature, see Claude Cahen, "Points de vue sur la 'Revolution 'abbaside,'" in *Revue Historique,* fasc. 468 (1963), 295–338. See further 'Abd al-'Azīz al-Dūrī, "*Ḍaw' jadīd 'alā 'l-da'wa al-'Abbāsiyya,*" in *Majallat kulliyyat al-ādāb wa'l-funūn* (Baghdad), 1960, 64–82; B. Lewis, "'Abbāsids," "'Alids," and "Hās͟himiyya," in *Enc. Islam,* 2nd ed.
11. G. van Vloten, "Zur Abbasidengeschichte," 220–2. The story of how the poet Muṭī' b. Iyās invented a hadith showing Mahdī to be the predestined heir to the Caliphate (*K. al-Aghānī,* Būlāq edition, xii, 85)

is regarded by Prof. G. van Grunebaum as doubtful: 'Three Arabic poets of the early Abbasid age,' in *Orientalia,* xvii (1948), 171. A verse ascribed to the contemporary poet Abū Dulāma refers to al-Manṣūr himself as the Mahdī. Ibn Qutayba, *Al-Ma'ārif,* 420; idem, *'Uyūn al-akhbār*, i, 26; Van Vloten, *Opkomst*, 66.

12. See H.F. Amedroz, "On the meaning of the *laqab* 'al-Saffāḥ" as applied to the first Abbasid Caliph,' in *JRAS,* (1907), 660–3.
13. Dūrī, *Al-'Aṣr al-'Abbāsī al-awwal,* Baghdad 1363/ 1945, 65–6; Tyan, *Institutions,* 489, n. 2.
14. Dūrī, loc. cit, where references are given.
15. Ṭabarī, iii, 30. Variant versions of the Kufa address appear in a number of other sources.
16. Dūrī, loc. cit, citing Ya'qūbī and the *K. al-Imāma wa'l-Siyāsa* attributed to Ibn Qutayba.
17. *Al-Akhbār al-ṭiwāl,* Cairo 1330, 351 ff; Dūrī 65.
18. Mas'ūdī, *Tanbīh,* 292; French translation, 434–5; Van Vloten, *Recherches ...,* 68.
19. *Rusūm,* 129; repeated by Qalqashandī in *Ṣubḥ*, v, 477 and *Ināfa*, i, 170.
20. *Die auf Südarabien bezüglichen Angaben Našwāns im Šams al-'Ulūm,* ed. Azimuddin Ahmad, Gibb Memorial series, xxiv, London-Leiden 1916, 103. Part of the passage in question was cited by D. H. Müller in his "Die Burgen und Schlösser Sudarabiens nach dem Iklîl des Hamdânî," in *Wiener Akad. Sitzungsberichte,* phil. hist. kl., xciv–xcvii (1879–81), 407–8, n. 6.
21. Ed. and German translation by Müller, "Die Burgen und Schlösser," 367–8 and 407; ed. Anastās al-Karmalī, Baghdad 1931, 71–2; abridged English translation,

Nabih Amin Faris, *The antiquities of South Arabia,* Princeton 1938, 41.

22. Ibn Khaldūn, *Muqaddima,* ed. E. Quatremère, ii, 147 and 158–9; English translation F. Rosenthal. New York 1958, ii, 164 and 179; Muṭahhar b. Ṭāhir al-Maqdisī, *K. al-Bad' wa'l-ta'rīkh,* ed. and French translation C. Huart, ii, Paris, 1899, 183–4; trans. 164; I. Goldziher, "Pinehas—Manṣūr," in *ZDMG,* lvi (1902), 411–2; A. Marmorstein, "Les signes du Messie," in *REJ,* lii (1906), 176–86; Snouck Hurgronje, 156.
23. Ṭabarī ii, 616; Balādhurī, *Ansāb al-ashrāf,* v, ed. S. D. F. Goitein. Jerusalem 1936, 225; Cf. G. C. Miles, "Al-Mahdī al-haqq, amīr al-mu'minīn," in *Revue Numismatique,* 6e series, vii (1965), 336, and Fariq, 78. Mr. M. Sharon points out to me that the same phrase occurs in Ibn A'tham al-Kūfī, *K. al-Futūḥ,* Ms. Ahmed III 2956, Topkapı Sarayı, Istanbul, ii 2a.
24. See for example J. Wellhausen, *Die religiös-politischen Oppositionsparteien im alten Islam (Abhandlungen der kgl. Ges. der Wiss. Göttingen, phil. hist. kl.,* N. S. v, 2). Berlin 1901, 90f; idem, *The Arab kingdom and its fall,* trans. Margaret Graham Weir, Calcutta 1927, 234, 245. On the connections between the movement of Mukhtār and the later pro-Abbasid movement, see Wellhausen, *Arab kingdom,* 504–5; S. Moscati, "Il testamento di Abu Hašım," in *RSO,* xxvii (1952), 44–6. On the importance of the South Arabian element in early Shi'ism, see W. Montgomery Watt, "Shi'ism under the Umayyads," in *JRAS* (1960), 158–72.
25. Mas'ūdī, *Tanbīh* 272: French translation 407: Maqdisī, *Bad',* ii 184; {Balādhurī}, *Anonyme arabische Chronik Band XI,* ed. W. Ahlwardt, Greifswald 1883, 334, citing some 'prophetic' verses; Van Vloten. *Recherches..* 61;

Wellhausen, *Arab kingdom,* 245 ff. Farazdaq sneers at the Yemenites of Kufa for following both Mukhtār and Ibn Ash'ath (cit. Wellhausen, 234, n.l.). A work by Abū Mikhnaf 'on the tradition *yā Himyara* and the death of Ibn Ash'ath' is mentioned in the *Fihrist* of Ibn al-Nadīm, ed. G. Flügel, Leipzig 1871, 93.

26. Ṭabarī, ii, 1676; Van Vloten, *Opkomst,* 61.
27. Ṭabarī, ii, 1972; Mas'ūdī, *Murūj,* vi, 61; Van Vloten, *Opkomst,* 61. On the eschatological and revolutionary significance of the black emblems in the Abbasid and some earlier risings, see Van Vloten. *Opkomst,* 132 ff.; *Recherches.* 63 ff.; Wellhausen *Arab Kingdom:* 533–4. See especially Ṭabarī, ii, 1929 f.
28. G.C. Miles, 'Al-Mahdī al-haqq', 329–30, 333–6, 339–40.
29. M.J. de Goeje, *Memoire sur les Carmathes* ... 2nd ed., Leiden 1886, 73; I. Friedlaender, 'The heterodoxies of the Shiites', in *JAOS,* xxix (1908), 109; B. Lewis, *The origins of Isma'ilism,* Cambridge 1940, 95.
30. The name al-Hādī (see G. van Vloten, Zur "Abbasidengeschichte," 222–4) seems to mark the transition from messianic to purely regnal titles. If Dr. Miles is right in this reading and interpretation of an undated silver dirham (op. cit. 330 and 337–8), it is possible that even the name al-Rashīd may have retained some broader religious implications.

Notes to Chapter 9

1. v, 58.
2. In Diodorus Siculus ii, 32; Cf. A. Christensen, *Heltedigtning og Fortællingslitteratur hos Iranerne i Oldtiden,* Copenhagen 1935, 69 ff.

3. V. Gardthausen, *Griechische Paläographie*, i, Leipzig 1911, 91 f.; M. Jastrow, *A Dictionary of the Targumim etc.*, New York 1926, 304.
4. N. Abbott, *Studies in Arabic Literary Papyri*, i, Chicago 1957, 21–24; Cf. Goldziher, *Muh.St.*, ii, 50–52 and 180–1. Stories of personal libraries and record collections in the first century A.H. must be treated with caution, Cf. the comments of J. Schacht on the spurious tradition of the archives of Kurayb, *On Mūsā b. 'Uqba's Kitāb al-Maghāzī, AO*, 1953, xxi, 296–7. On the earliest Arabic papyrus quires see A. Grohmann, "The Value of Arabic Papyri," *Proc. of the Royal Soc. of Hist. Studies*, i, Cairo 1951, 43 ff.
5. See A. Grohmann, "New discoveries in Arabic Papyri. An Arabic Tax-Account Book," *Bulletin de l'Institut Egyptien,* xxxii, 1949–50, 159–170.
6. Cf. Ibn al-Nadīm, *Fihrist,* 21.
7. *Ta'rīkh-i Qumm* 180.
8. *Ta'rīkh,* ii, 258.
9. A.K.S. Lambton, *Landlord and Peasant in Persia*, London 1953, 15 n.1.
10. *Futūḥ* 450; ed. Cairo 1901, 455.
11. Ṭabarī, ii, 1957, 1969; see further N. Fries, *Das Heerwesen der Araber zur Zeit der Omaijaden,* 1921, 9; W. Hoenerbach, "Zur Heeresverwaltung der Abbasiden," *Isl.,* xxix, 1949–50, 263.
12. Fol. 45 b; ed. Cairo 89.
13. *Khiṭaṭ,* i, 91.
14. Papyrus rolls (?), Cf. Qalqashandī, *Ṣubḥ,* i, 423—*adrāj min kāghidh waraq*.
15. Fol. 79 b; ed. Cairo 138.
16. W. Björkman, *Beiträge zur Geschichte der Staatskanzlei im islamischen Ägypten,* Hamburg 1928, 7;

A. Grohmann, *From the World of Arabic Papyri,* Cairo 1952, 23 ff., 45 ff., 52; *Corpus Papyrorum Raineri Archiducis Austriae,* iii, *Series Arabica,* ed. A. Grohmann, i/I, *Allgemeine Einführung in die arabischen Papyri,* Vienna 1924, 32 ff., 54 ff., etc.

17. Described by A. Grohmann, *New Discoveries..,* and idem, *New Discoveries..* II, *BIE,* xxxv, 1952–3, 159–169.
18. See below.
19. On *Awāraj* see V. Minorsky in his edition of *Tadhkirat al-Mulūk,* London 1943, 144; to be modified in the light of W. Hinz, *Rechnungswesen,* 120 ff.
20. This seems to be the meaning of *aṣl* and *istikhrāj,* rather than income and expenditure, as assumed by Cevdet and Uzunçarşılı. On *istikhrāj* in the sense of revision Cf. Uzunçarşılı, *Medhal,* 278 and Hinz, *Rechnungswesen* 18, On *Aṣl* Cf. Māwardī, *al-Aḥkām al-Sulṭāniyya,* ed. Enger 373, ed. Cairo 209. The expression *dafātir-i aṣl wa-istikhrāj* occurs in a text from Seljuk Anatolia—O. Turan, *Türkiye Selcukları hakkında Resmi Vesikalar,* Ankara 1958, text xxvi.
21. cf. "*'amal*" in Dozy, *Suppl.* ii, 175.
22. Khwārizmī, *Mafātīḥ al-'Ulūm,* ed. Van Vloten, 54–8, Cf. Mez, *Renaissance,* 103, Eng. tr. 109, where however Mez's meaning is not very clearly rendered. An abridged Turkish paraphrase of Khwārizmī's text was made, in the light of Ottoman bureaucratic experience, by M. Cevdet, *Defter,* 88–91; there is also a rather more rapid Turkish summary by I. H. Uzunçarşılı, *Osmanlı Devleti Teşkilâtına Medhal,* Istanbul 1941, 479–480. This last has been translated into German by B. Spuler, *Iran in früh-islamischer Zeit,* Wiesbaden 1952, 338 n. 1.

23. This would seem to be the meaning of the term *Qānūn* in Māwardī, *Al-Aḥkām al-Sulṭāniyya,* ed. Enger 370, ed. Cairo 207.
24. M. Minovi and V. Minorsky, *Naṣīr al-Dīn Ṭūsī on Finance, BSOAS,* x, 1940, 761, 773, 781; Hinz, *Rechnungswesen,* 134ff.
25. Grohmann, *New Discoveries..,* 163.
26. *Khiṭaṭ*, i, 82.
27. For specimens of land-tax registers from Egypt, on papyrus rolls, see A. Dietrich, *Arabische Papyri,* Leipzig 1937, 81 ff.
28. Muḥammad b. Yaḥyā al-Ṣūlī, *Adab al-Kātib,* Cairo 1341, 193.
29. A Christian treasury official, appointed head of the *Dīwān al-jahbadha* in the following year—'Arīb, *Tab. Cont.* 135; on him see also Ṣūlī, *Akhbār al-Rāḍī* 199; Hilāl al-Sābī, *Wuzarā',* 136, 279, 296.
30. *Tajārib al-Umam,* ed. Amedroz, i, 151–2.
31. Ibid., 155 and 164. The rendering of these passages in the English translation of Miskawayh by D.S. Margoliouth does not bring out their technical significance.
32. *Ta'rīkh-i Qumm,* 149ff.; Cf. Ann K.S. Lambton, "An Account of the Tarikhi Qumm," *BSOAS,* xii, 1948, 595; C. Cahen, *Quelques problèmes économiques et fiscaux de l'Iraq Buyide … AIEO,* x, 1952, 355. On the *Rūznāmaj* see further F. Løkkegaard, *Islamic Taxation in the Classic Period,* Copenhagen 1950, 149 and 159.
33. *Kitāb Qawānīn al-Dawāwīn,* ed. A.S. Atiya, Cairo 1943, 304. For examples of *Rūznāmaj* from Egypt see Grohmann, *New Discoveries..;* for a discussion of the systems of accountancy they reveal, C. Leyerer, "Die Verrechnung und Verwaltung."

34. Fol. 179a–182b; ed. 281–8.
35. *Muq. i,* 321–4 = Rosenthal, i, 361–5. See further R. Levy, *The Social Structure of Islam*, Cambridge 1957, 317–320. A budget for 306/908 is given by Hilāl, *Wuzarā'*, 11–22, and was analyzed, together with other sources, by A. von Kremer, "Über das Einnahmebudget des Abbasiden-Reiches," *Denkschrift d. Phil. hist. Kl. d. Wiener Ak.*, xxxvi, 1888, 283–362. A statement of the revenues of the privy purse (*Bayt māl al-Khāṣṣa*) in the 4th/10th century is given by Miskawayh (Mez 115–6).
36. Tr. Wüstenfeld, in *Das Heerwesen der Muhammedaner*, Göttingen 1880, 1–7. Both are examined, with other evidence, by W. Hoenerbach, *Zur Heereserwaltung* ... 269 ff.
37. Qalqashandī *Ṣubḥ*, vi, 492–3 = Wüstenfeld, *Die Geographie und Verwaltung von Ägypten*, Göttingen 1879, 190–1.
38. ed. 'Alī Bahjat, Cairo 1905, 137–141, Fr. trans. by H. Massé in *BIFAO*, xi, 1914, 104–8; Cf. Qalqashandī, *Ṣubḥ., i,* 133–5, where they are given in a slightly different order, and Björkman, *Beiträge*, 24–5.
39. Translated by Massé as 'bulletin.'
40. *Ṣubḥ*, i, 139, Cf. Björkman, *Beiträge*, 39.
41. See for example Juwaynī, i, 24–5 = Boyle, i, 33–4, and Rashīd al-Dīn, *Jāmi' al-Tawārīkh,* ed. Blochet, 39–40, 56–7; Cf. ibid. 483 on the *daftars* of Pekin.
42. ed. N. Lugal and A.S. Erzi, part 1; Ankara 1937; abridgment, Houtsma, *Recueil,* ii; German trans. H. W. Duda, Copenhagen 1959; Turkish adaptation by Yazijioghlu 'Alī, Houtsma, *Recueil*, iii.
43. Ibn Bībī, 146, Antalya; 153–4, Sinop; 428, Akhlāṭ.
44. *Recueil,* iii 105—not in Ibn Bībī.

45. Ibn Bībī 127.
46. *Recueil*, iii, 109. For similar appointments to the *dīwān al-ᶜarḍ* by Sanjar see *K. 'Atabat al-Kataba*, eds. Muḥ. Qazwīnī and 'Abbās Iqbāl, Tehran 1329, 39–40, 72–3.
47. *Recueil*, iii, 210.
48. Pp. 254–5.
49. Cevdet 91–3.
50. "Moğollar devrinde Anadolu'nun Iktisadi Vaziyeti," *THITM*, i, 1931, 1–42.
51. W. Hinz, *Ein orientalisches Handelsunternehmen im* 15 *Jahrhundert, Welt des Orients*, 1949, 313–40.
52. *Die Resalä-ye Falakiyyä*, Wiesbaden 1952.
53. For a full discussion of these registers, and of the variations in usage and nomenclature, see Hinz, *Rechnungswesen*, 113–137.
54. For a description of their material form see L. Fekete, *Die Siyaqat-Schrift*, i, 70 ff.

Notes to Chapter 10

1. Ch. 31; ed. N. Atsız, *Osmanlı tarihleri*, Istanbul 1949, 118; German trans. R. Kreutel, *Vom Hirtenzeit zur hohen Pforte*, Graz 1959, 66.
2. Quoted by Ibn Ḥajar in the *Inbā' al-ghumr, anno* 805; Şevkiye Inalcık, *Ibn Hacer'de Osmanlı'lara dair haberler*, in *AÜDTCFD*, vi/3, (1948), 192, 195; Cf. Tashköprüzāde Kemāl al-Dīn Meḥmed, *Ta'rīkh-i Ṣāf*, Istanbul 1287, 34.
3. Ch. 81; text 155–6, tr. 134.
4. Ch. 122; text 190–1, tr. 195.
5. Solaḳzāde, *Ta'rīkh*, 268; Muṣṭafā Nūrī Pasha, *Netā'ij al-wuḳū'āt*[2], i, Istanbul 1327, 59; ᶜAbd al-Rahmān

Sheref, "Topḳapı Sarāy-i humāyūnu," in *TOEM*, i/6, 1911, 351.

6. *Ḳānūnnāme* 23.
7. Koču Bey, *Risāle*, ch. 2, ed. A.K. Aksüt, Istanbul 1939, 20–3; German trans. By W.F.A. Behrnauer in *ZDMG*, xv, (1861), 275 ff. Cf. Hammer-Purgstall, *GOR*, iii, 489; *Histoire*, vi 282.
8. *Ḳānūnnāme* 13, 23.
9. Ibid. 27.
10. *Munshe'āt al-Selāṭīn*², i, 595.
11. Ed. Greaves 1747, 616.
12. On these two see I.H. Uzunçarşılı, *Osmanlı devleti teşkilâtından kapıkulu ocakları*, i, Ankara 1943, index, and idem, *Osmanlı devletinin saray teşkılâtı*, Ankara 1945, 225–9.
13. On these buildings, see 'Abd al-Rahmān Sheref, "Topḳapı-Sarāy-i humāyūnu."

Notes to Chapter 11

1. Fārābī *Arā' ahl al-madīna al-fāḍila*, ed. Dieterici, Leiden 1895, 62; E.I.J. Rosenthal, *Political thought in medieval Islam*, Cambridge 1938, 136, 278; F. Rosenthal, *The Muslim Concept of Freedom*, Leiden 1960, 100–1.
2. *E.g.*, Nāmik Kemāl in *Ḥürriyyet*, 14 September 1868, cited by Şerif Mardin, *The Genesis of Young Ottoman Political Thought*, Princeton 1962, 296–7; Agaoghlu Aḥmed, in *Khilāfet we millī ḥākimiyyet*, Ankara 1339 [= 1923], 22 ff.; Rashīd Riḍā, *Al-Khilāfa*, Cairo 1341, 5, tr. in H.Z. Nuseibeh, *The Ideas of Arab Nationalism*, Cornell 1956, 125.
3. *Ṣubḥ*. viii, 46–8.

4. Cf. J.F. Ruphy. *Dictionnaire abrégé français-arabe*, Paris, an X [1802], 185.
5. *Lubnān fī 'ahd al-umarā' al-Shihābiyyīn,* Beirut, 1933, ii, 218–9 etc.
6. ii, 222–4.
7. Cited *op. cit.* 213 n. 1fi
8. *'Ajā'ib*, iii, 5, etc.; *Maẓhar al-taqdīs* ed. Cairo n.d. i, 37.
9. See for example 'Āṭif Efendi's memorandum of 1798 in Jevdet, *Ta'rīkh*², vi, 395, speaking of 'equality and republicanism'—*müsāwāt we-jümhūriyyet*; the documents on the Septinsular republic (*Jezā'ir-i Seb'a-i Müjtemi'a Jümhūru*) of 1799 published by I.H. Uzunçarşılı in *Belleten*, i, 1937, 633,—*jümhūriyyet wejhīle ijtimā'*; the dispatches of Ḥālet Efendi from Paris in E.Z. Karal, *Halet Efendinin Paris Büyük Elçiliği* (1802–06), Istanbul 1940, 35; Cf. 'Āṣim, *Ta'rīkh,* i, 61–2, 78–9, and the Turkish translation of Botta's *Storia d'Italia*, Cairo 1249/1834, repr. Istanbul 1293/1876, passim. Shaykh Rifā'a Rāfi' al-Ṭahṭāwī (*Talkhīṣ al-ibrīz*), Būlāq 1834, Ch. 5 = Cairo ed. 1958, 252–3) uses *jumhūriyya* in both senses.
10. See for example the instructive comments of 'Alī Su'āwī in 1876 on the 'true meaning' of *jumhūr*, cited in M.C. Kuntay, *Ali Suavi*, Istanbul 1946, 95, tr. in Ş. Mardin, *op. cit.*, 382–3. It is probably in this sense that the term is used of the Lebanese peasant rebels led by Ṭanyūs Shāhīn: see Yūsuf Ibrāhīm Yazbak, *Thawra wa-fitna fī Lubnān*, Damascus 1938, 87; Eng. trans. M.H. Kerr, *Lebanon in the last years of feudalism..*, Beirut 1959, 53; Cf. Ra'īf al-Khūrī, *Al-fikr al-'arabī al- ḥadīth*, Beirut 1943, 94.
11. Documents in 'A. K. Gharā'iba, *Dirāsāt fī ta'rīkh Ifriqiya al-'Arabiyya*, Damascus 1960, 105 ff.

12. For texts and debates see A. S. Gözübüyük and S. Kili, *Türk Anayasa metinleri*, Ankara 1957, 95 f.; K. Ariburnu, *Millî Mücadele ve inkılâplarla ilgili kanunlar*, i, Ankara 1957, 32 ff.; Cf. E. Smith, "Debates on the Turkish Constitution of 1924," in *Ankara Üniv. Siyasal Bilg. Fak. Derg.*, xiii (1958), 82–105.

Notes to Chapter 12

1. On loan-words, see further Charles Issawi, "European Loan-Words in Contemporary Arabic Writing: A Case Study in Modernization," in *Middle Eastern Studies*, iii (1967), pp. 110–33.
2. See *Encyclopaedia of Islam*, 2nd edition, under "Djumhūriyya." The term *mashyakha* is still used for "republic" in an Arabic translation of Machiavelli's *Prince,* made for Muhammad 'Alī Pasha in about 1825. This text, a manuscript of which exists in the Egyptian National Library, is of considerable interest for the history of modern Arabic political terminology and deserves a critical edition.
3. Midhat Cemal Kuntay, *Sarıklı ihtilâlci Alî Suavi* (Istanbul, 1964), pp. 58–59; Şerif Mardin, *The Genesis of Young Ottoman Thought* (Princeton, N. J., 1962), p. 372.
4. Mehmet Akif Ersoy, "Hakkın sesleri," in *Safahat,* 6th ed. (Istanbul, 1963), pp. 205–206; B. Lewis, *The Middle East and the West* (London and Bloomington, Ind., 1964), p. 89. Revised edition: *The Shaping of the Modern Middle East* (New York and Oxford, 1994), p. 88.

5. Ahmed Naim, *Islâmda dava-yı kavmiyet* (Istanbul, 1913), cited by Niyazi Berkes in *The Development of Secularism in Turkey* (Montreal, 1964), pp. 374–75.
6. U. Heyd, *Foundations of Turkish Nationalism* (London, 1950), p. 60; *cf.* Ziya Gökalp, *Turkish Nationalism and Western Civilization*, translated and edited by Niyazi Berkes (London, 1959), pp. 79 ff., 97 ff., 113 ff., 126 ff.
7. C. Ernest Dawn, "Ideological Influences in the Arab Revolt," in *The World of Islam: Studies in Honour of Philip* K. *Hitti,* ed. James Kritzeck and R. Bayly Winder (London, 1959), p. 240, citing *Revue du Monde musulman*, xlvii (1921), pp. 24–27 of Arabic text, 15–20 of translation.
8. See *Encyclopaedia of Islam,* 2nd edition, s.v.v.
9. See Ḥasan al-Bāshā, *Al-Alqāb al-Islāmiyya fi'l-ta'rīkh wa'l-wathā'iq wa'l-āthār* (Cairo, 1957), pp. 310–11; R. Dozy, *Supplément aux dictionnaires arabes*, 2nd ed. (Leiden-Paris, 1927), i, p. 593; additional examples in Abū Shāma, *Tarājim rijāl al-qarnayn al-sādis wa'l-sābi', ed.* Muḥ. Zāhid al-kawtharī (Cairo, 1947), p. 81; Ibn al-Fuwaṭī, *Al-Ḥawādith al-jāmi'a*, ed. Muṣṭafā Jawād (Baghdad, A.H. 1351), p. 218; Ibn al-'Adīm, ed. B. Lewis, in *Arabica,* xiii (1966), p. 266.
10. See above, p. 320; also B. Lewis, *The Emergence of Modern Turkey*, 2nd edition (London, 1968), p. 156; Ş. Mardin, *The Genesis of Young Ottoman Thought*, pp. 23, 215.
11. In classical usage this was a legal, occasionally a social, but never a political term. On its modern development see *Encyclopaedia of Islam*, 2nd edition, s.v. "Ḥurriyya."